Your Opinion, *Please!*

Second Edition

Dedication

*To Michael, Paula, Chelsea, Cameron, Dylan, Lindsay,
Jessica, Emily, Justin, Allison, Nicole, Audrey, and Jack.
May you grow up learning to ask the right questions.*

*And to the thousands of committed educators everywhere
who have gained the wisdom of asking the right
questions and heeding the answers.*

Second Edition

Your Opinion, Please!

How to Build
the Best
Questionnaires
in the Field
of Education

James Cox ● Keni Brayton Cox

CORWIN PRESS
A SAGE Company
Thousand Oaks, CA 91320

For information:

Corwin Press
A SAGE Company
2455 Teller Road
Thousand Oaks, California 91320
www.corwinpress.com

SAGE Ltd.
1 Oliver's Yard
55 City Road
London EC1Y 1SP
United Kingdom

SAGE India Pvt. Ltd.
B 1/I 1 Mohan Cooperative
    Industrial Area
Mathura Road, New Delhi 110 044
India

SAGE Asia-Pacific Pte. Ltd.
33 Pekin Street #02-01
Far East Square
Singapore 048763

Library of Congress Cataloging-in-Publication Data

Cox, James (James B.)
Your opinion, please! : how to build the best questionnaires in the field of education/by James Cox, Keni B. Cox. —2nd ed.
    p. cm.
Includes bibliographical references and index.
ISBN 978-1-4129-5538-6 (cloth)
ISBN 978-1-4129-5539-3 (pbk.)
    1. Education—Research. 2. Questionnaires—Design.
3. Educational surveys—Design. I. Cox, Keni B. II. Title.

LB1028.C67 2008
370.72—dc22   2007031659

This book is printed on acid-free paper.

07   08   09   10   11   10 9   8   7   6   5   4   3   2   1

Acquisitions Editor:	Rachel Livsey
Managing Editor:	Debra Stollenwerk
Editorial Assistants:	Jordan Barbakow, Allison Scott
Production Editor:	Veronica Stapleton
Copy Editor:	Linda Gray
Typesetter:	C&M Digitals (P) Ltd.
Proofreader:	Doris Hus
Indexer:	Kathleen Paparchontis
Cover Designer:	Monique Hahn

Contents

Acknowledgments

This, the second edition of *Your Opinion, Please!* would not have been possible without the first edition, now a near relic of the past century. In the 1996 edition, I acknowledged Lillian Wehmeyer, PhD, noted author (now deceased) for her initial editing. Also I made note of the incredible students and staff of the Department of Organizational Management at the University of La Verne, California, for paving the road that led me to learning how to do this work. I continue to value the contribution of these individuals.

Currently, as an "almost retiree," I continue to be grateful to those who relay to me (and others) the professional "aha!" that resulted when they came to realize just how important it is to create high-quality questionnaires as one part of our data-obsessed culture. There are so many ways that they have communicated this newly discovered awareness, which boils down to this: "Poor questionnaires lead to inaccurate data, which leads to wrong decisions, which leads to wasteful expenditures of time, money, and energy. . . all of this because of a poorly constructed questionnaire." A small exaggeration perhaps, but I acknowledge these professionals and their aha's! nonetheless.

—Jim

A special thanks to Corey Greenlaw, EdD, Fresno County Office of Education, California, for his generous gift of time in advising and reviewing our inclusion of Web-based surveying. Additionally, much appreciation is due the faculty and students in the Educational Leadership Department, College of Education at California State University, Fullerton. Particular recognition is due Dr. Louise Adler, Dr. Ron Oliver, and Dr. Ken Stichter for their support and cheerful assistance to this new colleague. Finally, to Jim—husband, colleague, and mentor—for the invitation to participate in a "quick" revision that became a five-month rewrite and for his inexhaustible attention to quality and detail.

—Keni

Corwin Press would like to thank the following peer reviewers for their editorial insight and guidance:

Ronald L. Russell
Associate Director
Loess Hills Area Education Agency 13
Shenandoah, Iowa

Aghop Der-Karabetian, PhD
Professor of Psychology
University of La Verne

Susan J. Thomas
Senior Management Consultant, IBM Global Business Services
Learning Consulting
Charlottesville, VA

About the Authors

 **James Cox** is currently semiretired, but the door is not quite closed. He has been a consultant, facilitator, and evaluator for school districts engaged in school restructuring, testing, and other forms of assessment and program evaluation. Cox has the special gift of being able to bring technical information to the layperson in a simple understandable manner. A native of Colorado, he credits the University of Northern Colorado (BA, 1960; MA, 1963; PhD, 1968) for providing him with the skills to teach and kindling within him a passion for education.

From 1996 to 2006, representing his and Keni's consulting firm, JK Educational Associates, he worked with schools and districts, primarily in California, in a variety of assessment and accountability areas. Prior to that he was on the faculty of the University of La Verne in Southern California (1993–1997) and served as Director of Research and Evaluation for the Anaheim Union High School District (1982–1990), as an evaluation consultant for the Los Angeles County Superintendent of Schools Office (1975–1982), and as a staff member for CTB McGraw-Hill (1970–1975).

He has one additional book, published in January 2007, Finding the Story Behind the Numbers: A Tool Based Guide for Evaluating Educational Programs.

 **Keni Brayton Cox** is Assistant Professor in the Department of Educational Leadership, College of Education, California State University, Fullerton. The majority of her students are practicing teachers and novice researchers working toward a master's of science in education and a credential in educational administration. She earned her PhD from the University of California, Riverside, in 1994. Keni was Assistant Superintendent, Instructional Services for the Whittier City School District (1997–2005) and Executive Director, Instructional Services, for the Riverside Unified School District (1992–1997). She coordinated the Administrative Training Center/California School Leadership Academy for the Riverside County Office of Education (1989–1992) and served as a staff development specialist, a high school teacher and a site administrator for the Anaheim Union High School District in Orange County, California.

Keni bases her educational philosophy on three platforms: professional collaboration, individual accountability, and a passion for reducing the predictability of academic achievement based on class, language, and ethnicity. Her primary research interest is the response of school district/central office leadership to the pressures of high-stakes accountability.

Introduction

Y*our Opinion, Please!* was originally published in 1996 and was well received among its intended audience: the novice researcher looking for a simple, comprehensive guide to developing effective questionnaires and the graduate student in need of simple directions. In the 10 years since the original publication, the demand for accurate information and for efficient ways of collecting data has increased in all arenas, and the field of education is no exception. Within the reality of high-stakes testing and the demands of accountability from almost every quarter, there are more questions than ever before. Along with the need for more information, we are faced with increasing choices on how to collect it. Hence, the need for this update.

The second edition of *Your Opinion, Please!* was undertaken in appreciation of twenty-first-century technology and the reality that the Internet is a new medium for researchers. Electronic surveying was relatively unknown 10 years ago; today, it is the first choice of many marketing companies. Along with the possibilities, however, are limitations and considerations, especially for those in the public sector. A primary purpose of this edition is to ensure that the graduate student or educational leader is well informed regarding both the potential and the possible pitfalls of Web-based questionnaire development and distribution.

Although a questionnaire is often the best means of collecting data for a particular research project, seldom do novice researchers (typically, graduate students or school- or district-based educators charged with organizing the data collection) have wide experience in questionnaire construction. And even less often is adequate time available to do a professional job.

This book, prepared with inexperienced and rushed questionnaire writers in mind, will help the reader construct a basic questionnaire, analyze the data, and then report the findings. The information in the manual is intentionally brief, concentrating on vital elements. Therefore, a novice writer can read it through quickly—and then, while working through the task, consult it as a reference.

On the other hand, for those who need to take the process a bit further, posed with satisfying a thesis or dissertation committee or other august group, this book is also for you. It's not just a primer.

Part I, consisting of Chapters 1–9, addresses the following essential stages of questionnaire development:

1. Establishing the guiding questions

2. Operationalizing the guiding questions

3. Writing items and formatting responses

4. Designing the questionnaire

5. Writing directions

6. Categorizing respondents

7. Conducting the alignment check

8. Validating the questionnaire

9. Marketing the questionnaire

Chapter 4, "Designing the Questionnaire," new to this edition, has been added as a separate chapter in recognition of the increasing body of research focusing on elements of design in questionnaire development.

Chapter 9, "Marketing the Questionnaire," includes research-based "hints" as to how to maximize response rates.

Whereas Chapters 1 through 9 lead the researcher through the stages of design and development of a quality questionnaire as simply and concisely as possible, Part II, entitled "Getting from Here to There," moves beyond basic design and delve into next steps and special considerations.

Chapters 10 and 11 discuss evaluation, analysis, and reporting of questionnaire data, and they reflect the technological advances of the twenty-first century.

Chapter 12, "To Web or Not to Web," is a discussion of the items to be considered when selecting the mode most appropriate to the researcher's purpose. Specific applications of the principles of Web-based design are outlined. Here, we hope *we* are asking the right questions!

Finally, Chapter 13, titled "Since You Asked . . ." addresses frequently asked questions regarding questionnaire development that are significant but were not included earlier in order to honor our promise of brevity.

Chapter 13 wraps up the directions and recommendations for building "the best questionnaires in the field of education." But there's more. Resources A through E, described below, are designed to reinforce and support the body of the text and, in part, to give your creative juices a boost.

Resource A, titled "Evaluating a Questionnaire: A Self Assessment," offers a tool for the questionnaire developer to assess the quality of his or her own instrument. Brief and very much to the point, Resource A is a checklist that reflects the content from Stages 1 through 8. Successfully passing the "test" of Resource A almost guarantees that your questionnaire has content validity. Resource A is designed to be copied and used every time you draft a new instrument.

How you introduce your instrument can encourage, or discourage, participation. Resource B, "Sample Introductions," contains examples of how to introduce a questionnaire effectively—that is, in a way that will encourage interest. You may have developed a beautiful questionnaire, but if few people choose to complete it, of what value is it? Resource B includes carefully worded introductions appropriate to typical educator groups, including teachers and parents.

Resource C, "Sample Directions and Formats," presents additional example of questionnaire formats and matching directions. Resource C is a reinforcement for Stages 4 and 5, "Designing the Questionnaire" and "Writing Directions," critical elements of a high-quality questionnaire, elements that are too frequently overlooked.

Resource D, "Critiquing Questionnaires: Finding Flaws," is a novel section that presents an example of a poorly constructed questionnaire and invites readers to see how many mistakes they can find. With Resource A as a guide, completing this activity provides a check of the reader's understanding. The example also works well as an icebreaker for questionnaire development seminars, the primary goal being to establish an informed and critical mind-set. Included in Resource D is the authors' critique.

Finally, Resource E, "Modeling the Product: From Guiding Questions to Alignment" models the entire questionnaire development process by introducing two scenarios, (a) professional development for educational leaders and (b) high school graduates' thoughts about their high school a year after graduation. For each scenario, the results of each step of questionnaire development are explained, providing a contextualized view of the entire process.

By applying the information in this book, new researchers will learn enough to graduate from novice to practitioner level. And they will find that they can do a thorough job in a relatively short period of time with a minimum of "woulda, shoulda, coulda."

Throughout, we have assumed that the research being conducted is based on good intentions and adherence to the principles that guide ethical research. For anyone questioning the appropriateness of a particular method or approach, two resources stand out: the American Psychological Association (APA) and the American Educational Research Association (AERA). The following preamble to Part II, "Research Populations, Educational Institutions, and the Public" of the Ethical Research Standards of the AERA provides a reference point:

> Educational researchers conduct research within a broad array of settings and institutions, including schools, colleges, universities, hospitals, and prisons. It is of paramount importance that educational researchers respect the rights, privacy, dignity, and sensitivities of their research populations and also the integrity of the institutions within which the research occurs. Educational researchers should be especially careful in working with children and other vulnerable populations. These standards are intended to reinforce and strengthen already existing standards enforced by institutional review boards and other professional associations. (Strike et al., 2002, p. 43)

Among the rights of participants detailed by the AERA are the rights to confidentiality, honesty between researcher and participants, and sensitivity to local policies and guidelines for conducting research (p. 44).

MODELING THE PROCESS OF QUESTIONNAIRE DEVELOPMENT

From time to time throughout this book, as the questionnaire evolves from Stage 1 through Stage 7, we will present parts of a prototype, or model, for the reader's consideration. Based on a scenario described in Stage 1, "Guiding Questions," the example used throughout deals with the leadership skills of school principals. Unless otherwise indicated, the particular segment of the model is shown *in italics* and simply suggests to the reader what that aspect of development might look like. The heading "Modeling the Process of Questionnaire Development" precedes each presentation. Resource E includes two additional examples to demonstrate Stages 1 through 7 of the questionnaire development process.

Part I

Stages of Questionnaire Development

1

Establishing the Guiding Questions

Guiding questions identify the kinds of information a questionnaire will be designed to address. This is the first stage of the process and guides development of the questionnaire. These "guiding questions," few in number, establish a focus. Questions may be as general as "What is the overall attitude of parents, teachers, and administrators toward the district's efforts to establish a standards-based mathematics program?" or as specific as "What are the perceived benefits and liabilities of using benchmark assessments in the classroom?"

Guiding questions are not the actual questions included in the questionnaire. Rather, these Stage 1 questions frame—or establish a context for—the instrument. A continuous focus on these questions helps the writer stay focused and avoid extraneous items.

Two criteria define the quality and utility of guiding questions: clarity and relevance. For educators seeking information about a particular issue, the guiding questions might begin with phrases such as these:

What are the teachers' and administrators' attitudes toward . . . ?

What do teachers see as priorities for . . . ?

Do various groups of parents differ in their views regarding . . . ?

To what degree is . . . being implemented as designed?

Do teachers and administrators respond differently regarding . . . ?

How effective is Program X according to teachers and administrators?

For graduate students using a questionnaire in a thesis or dissertation, the guiding questions in Stage 1 of questionnaire construction are likely to be the research questions for which a questionnaire is designed.

In the absence of previously identified research questions, the process for establishing the guiding questions may be as commonplace as gathering a group of individuals together, brainstorming and setting priorities on the important issues, and then formulating the questions as suggested above. Sometimes a more formal process is required. For example, if a school or district is facing a difficult and sensitive issue, such as school boundary changes or teen drug use, formal inquiry of selected stakeholders is desirable to determine the questions that will frame the work ahead. In this case, bringing a small homogeneous group together to settle on the questions will not do the job. Similarly, a graduate student preparing for a thesis or dissertation should not attempt to establish the questions informally. Quite likely, the student's academic committee would be the group of choice.

When a formal process is called for, three sources may help frame the guiding questions:

1. Dialoguing with colleagues and significant stakeholders

2. Reviewing the literature to see what specialists in the field say about the issue

3. Consulting directly with three or four experts in the field to obtain their insights

NOTE: The success of the entire inquiry rests on the **clarity** and **relevance** of the questions. Do not take this step lightly! Finding answers to the guiding questions is the whole purpose of creating the questionnaire.

MODELING THE PROCESS OF QUESTIONNAIRE DEVELOPMENT

Scenario: School principals are currently being asked to assume greater responsibility than perhaps ever before. They are accountable for meeting a variety of local, state, and federal mandates, and the quality of student outcomes has been placed squarely on their shoulders. Within this context, School District X, a growing district, currently with 17 schools, wishes to conduct a needs assessment in regard to site leadership. They want to know, through the eyes of the teachers, the kinds of leadership skills most important for building excellent schools and the level of performance of the district's current principals relative to these skills.

The activity is supported by both principals and teachers, as it has been made clear that this is not an evaluation activity. No individual site data shall be reported. Those collecting the data will not be able to connect the information with any single principal. The results will be considered along with input from other sources to build a professional development program "second to none" for the district's current and prospective principals. The latter group is particularly important as the district anticipates the need to hire a minimum of nine site administrators within the next three years due to growth and retirement.

It was determined through administrative group consensus that the following questions would guide the study:

1. *What are the perceptions of our teachers relative to principals' performance on a selected set of leadership skills?*

2. *Are there differences in responses according to (a) school level (elementary or secondary) or (b) years at the same school?*

3. *Of the skills listed, which do teachers believe are the most important to address; that is, which skills are foundational to the new leadership training program?*

2

Operationalizing the Guiding Questions

Creating Specificity

Operationalizing the guiding questions improves the clarity of the questions identified in Stage 1 and is an important second stage in creating a high-quality instrument. It is crucial in the questionnaire development process that the general Stage 1 guiding questions become very specific in Stage 2. Often, the Stage 1 questions are quite general and may contain "fuzzy" words that need definition. Consider, for example, these words and phrases: standards-based instruction, school reform, accountability, self-concept, leadership skills, classroom management, attitude toward school, or standards-based portfolios. Words or phrases such as these are common as one reviews Stage 1 questions, but operationalizing or making such words clear is essential if the guiding questions are to "come alive," become observable.

To see this more clearly, the reader might consider the process as analogous to an inverted funnel. The small opening at the top represents a single guiding question (Stage 1). The opening at the bottom of the funnel represents expansion of the question to evoke meaningful, detailed responses. Assume that a Stage 1 question inquires about students' "attitudes toward school." This elusive but important concept undoubtedly would be viewed differently by various educators. If each educator were to construct a questionnaire to assess students' attitudes toward school, there probably would be as many different ways to spell out the concept as there were educators in the group. Therefore, if an instrument assessing students' attitudes toward school is to be administered, the group must operationalize exactly which observable characteristics make up "attitude."

For example, assume that student attitude toward school was defined by the group as the following:

- Regular attendance
- Completion of school work
- Behavior in class

5

- Expressed positive feelings about school
- Participation in class discussion
- Participation in extracurricular activities

For this activity, from this moment on, attitude toward school shall be clarified by assessing regular attendance + completion of school work + behavior in class + expressed positive feelings about school + participation in class discussion + participation in extracurricular activities. You may completely disagree with this list, but for now, this is it. This is what the group defined it to be. At this point, Stage 2 is complete.

Figuratively, the funnel relationship between Stage 1 guiding questions and Stage 2 clarifications might resemble the illustration in Figure 2.1.

Operational terms possess three characteristics: (a) They are observable, (b) they are limited only to important issues, and (c) they have the same level of specificity.

Operationalizing the guiding questions is not a "quick-and-careless" activity. It entails far more than simply thinking about the Stage 1 questions, then jotting down a few specifics. At the very least, operationalizing or making Stage 1 questions clear-cut involves obtaining input from at least three sources:

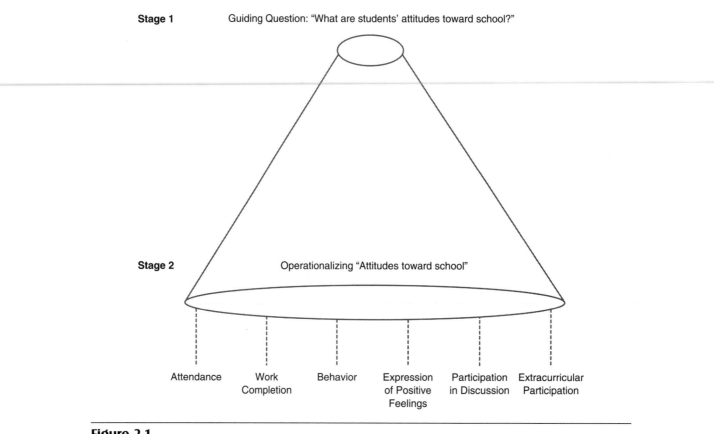

Figure 2.1

- The research literature: How has previous research defined your area of focus?

- Specialists in the particular area of interest: What is the position of these folks that will help avoid omissions, misinterpretations, or both?

- Dialogue among colleagues: How will local conditions be represented in your questionnaires?

MODELING THE PROCESS OF QUESTIONNAIRE DEVELOPMENT

Guiding Question 1 asked, *What are the perceptions of our teachers relative to principals' performance on a selected set of leadership skills?*

The "fuzzy" phrase in this question is "leadership skills." If the phrase "leadership skills" is used in a questionnaire item without further clarification, individual respondents undoubtedly would view that concept in different ways. If a report states that "62% of the respondents indicated a lack of leadership skills in their respective principals," just exactly what do the data mean? If one teacher views leadership skills in one way and another views them in another, what can we gain from these results? Thus it becomes necessary to identify *observable* characteristics or to *operationalize* leadership skills in some other way and to use those specific characteristics in the questionnaire items rather than the general term *leadership*. In using the more specific terms, we hope that respondents will remain focused, thinking about similar meanings for each issue.

Scenario (continued): Knowing that "leadership skills" must be made more specific, the staff in District X decides to conduct three focus groups locally, one composed of principals, one of teachers, and one a combined group. Additionally, three members of the leadership team volunteered to search the literature and compile a list of their discoveries. From there, the characteristics to be used for the questionnaire will be determined. When all this had been accomplished, the following list was endorsed:

1. *Establishes and communicates a vision for the organization*

2. *Plans effectively for implementing school programs*

3. *Demonstrates effective oral communication skills*

4. *Communicates effectively with others in writing*

5. *Establishes positive rapport with teachers*

6. *Maintains strong relationships with parents*

7. *Maintains positive rapport with students*

8. *Mediates disagreements effectively*

9. *Uses exemplary processes for the supervision and evaluation of instructional staff*

10. *Monitors the implementation of instructional programs effectively*

11. *Promotes and guides the use of technology by school staff*

12. *Solves problems effectively*

13. *Promotes and supports collaborative processes*

14. *Delegates and gives clear authority to complete tasks in a timely manner*

15. *Ensures a positive environment for teaching and learning*

The staff from District X determined that the questionnaire would be developed using the above list. Therefore, Stage 2 for the model questionnaire closes with "leadership skills" having been defined or operationalized by these 15 specific items.

3

Writing Items and Formatting Responses

S tage 3 involves the actual writing and formatting of the specific questionnaire items. A questionnaire is useful only to the extent that it collects accurate information. And for data to be accurate, questionnaire items must be precise rather than open to various interpretations. If items are precisely written, with as much specificity as possible, the responses will reflect the writer's actual intent in the questions, not what the respondent thinks the intent is.

Specificity improves the chance that the respondent will need to read each item only once. This decreases the time required to complete the form, reduces potential respondent frustration, and helps ensure the questionnaire's completion and prompt return. The list of suggestions beginning on this page and extending to page 15, with accompanying examples, covers significant points to remember when writing questionnaire items. As a general rule, when in doubt about item construction, terminology, or any other aspect of a certain question, put yourself in the place of the person who will be responding. Forget writing for a moment and focus on how the item reads. Any unclear item or a poorly formatted section that goes out to the respondent is a mistake that cannot be corrected.

ITEM WRITING

Following are several guidelines to help the reader write clear, unambiguous questionnaire items. To illustrate the points made, each suggestion is followed by one or more negative examples and an improved version of the same item.

1. Use simple sentence construction and word order.

> NOT: *What in your estimation are the strong points and the drawbacks to the reading program currently being implemented, as opposed to the proposed program for next year?*

9

INSTEAD: *What are the strengths and weaknesses of the current reading program?*

NOT: *When you consider what you will do after graduating from high school, what is the likelihood that you will further your education at a four-year college?*

INSTEAD: *Do you believe you will attend a four-year college next year?*

2. Write in the respondents' vocabulary. Avoid using uncommon terminology, jargon, or words or phrases with ambiguous meaning.

   NOT: *Do you believe that your child is progressing in the affective domain at XYZ School?*

   INSTEAD: Do *you believe that your child's social skills are progressing satisfactorily at XYZ School ?*

Affective is a term that means different things to different teachers and possibly means nothing at all to parents. The rephrased example, although not exactly duplicating the original in meaning, is an appropriate question for parents. Consider the respondent when choosing words. REMEMBER: Write in the vocabulary of the respondent.

   NOT: Do you believe that your principal is supportive?

   INSTEAD: *Does your principal provide resources needed for instruction?*

Supportive is a word whose definition varies. While a positive word, when one teacher says that the principal is supportive, it may not mean the same as when another teacher says the same thing. Being more specific, even if lengthier, is better than using a word or phrase that is open to multiple interpretations. Tell the respondent what you mean.

3. Avoid asking for respondents' opinions on a subject they cannot be expected to know anything about. Consider the respondents' frame of reference.

   NOT (for parents): *How do you rate the quality of the reading program at your Grade 5 child's school?*

   INSTEAD (For parents): *Are you satisfied with your child's progress in reading?*

Parents cannot be expected to know the criteria for evaluating a reading program, but they certainly know how they feel about their child's progress in reading.

4. Avoid "hard" or "soft" words and phrases (words or phrases with extreme connotations, either positive or negative).

These terms tend to attract or repel responses, not because of the content, but because of the word or phrase. Hard words tend to repel; soft words, attract. Moreover, some soft words result in little more than rhetorical questions, which generally have no place in questionnaires.

NOT: *Do you believe that state politicians should have a voice in determining the school curriculum?*

INSTEAD: *Do you believe that elected officials at the state level deserve a voice in determining the school curriculum?*

"State politicians" is a hard phrase and can elicit a negative response, regardless of what the respondent believes in regard to this issue. The rephrased question should provoke a more thoughtful answer since it is worded with a more neutral voice. In other words, do not lead respondents, encouraging them through your choice of words to give a particular answer.

NOT: *Do you believe the program intended to build the self-confidence and self-esteem of our students is a good idea?*

INSTEAD (for teachers): *Do you believe the "Students Come First" program currently being implemented at our school is working well?*

How can anyone be against a confidence-building, self-esteem–enhancing program? These are soft phrases that tend to attract responses. While the NOT/INSTEAD questions here are not the same (good idea vs. working well), we hope you see that the words used, regardless of what is being assessed, can affect the tendency of the respondents to mark one way or the other.

5. Avoid including more than one item in a single question.

NOT: *Were the two workshops on the language arts and math curricula effective?*

INSTEAD: *Was the workshop on the language arts curriculum effective?*

Was the workshop on the mathematics curriculum effective?

Perhaps the respondent found one workshop worthwhile and the other a waste of time. A compound question does not allow for different opinions on each part.

6. Couch sensitive questions in very careful language. Try to avoid questions in which the respondent indicts himself or herself with a negative response. Phrase statements so that it is okay for the respondent to give the socially non-desirable response.

NOT: *Do you use the procedures prescribed in our district for benchmark assessments?*

INSTEAD: *The steps for using benchmark assessments are listed below. You have probably used some and not others. Check those you have used.*

This is a sensitive question because not using the procedures would be an admission that the person is "not doing what I am supposed to do." Thus answering "yes" to the first question is the socially desirable response. Our recommendation is that you introduce the item in a way that makes "no" an OK response.

7. When a question calls for a "yes" or "no" answer, be sure you can interpret the meaning of a negative response.

> NOT: *When you give tests, do you like using performance assessments better than bubbled answer sheets?*

> INSTEAD: *When you give tests, do you like using performance assessments better than bubbled answer sheets? If NO, explain why not.*

A "no" answer could mean "I dislike them both," "I like bubbled answer sheets better," or "I like them both equally." A negative response can have multiple meanings. Without an explanation, therefore, the only way a definite conclusion can be drawn is from positive responses.

SCALAR RESPONSE ITEMS

Scales are very common in questionnaires, so it is important for developers to know a few basic details about them.

8. Make sure that responses match the stem. Generally speaking, there are two types of scales: intensity and frequency/amount scales. Intensity scales report the strength of feeling. Words such as *strongly, definitely,* and *very,* accompanied by a descriptor such as *agree* or *satisfied* express how strong the respondent feels about something. Frequency/amount scales report how often or how much of an event occurs: *A lot, often, rarely, once in a while, frequently,* and *some* are such descriptors.

> a. Intensity of feeling
> I have strong feelings about . . .
> I do not have strong feelings about . . .

Or

> I am very satisfied with . . .
> I am not at all satisfied with . . .

> b. Amount of something
> A great deal of . . . occurred.
> Not much of . . . occurred.

Or

> This almost always happens.
> This very rarely happens.

NOTE: A very common error in item writing is to supply the wrong scale for a stem—for example, using an intensity scale combined with a stem calling for an amount.

> NOT (on a *strongly agree* to *strongly disagree* scale): *I have implemented a standards-based reading program in my classroom.*

> INSTEAD (on a *fully implemented* to *not implemented* scale): *To what extent have you implemented a standards-based reading program in your classroom?*

In the "NOT" example above, what is the difference between *strongly agree* and *agree*? "I strongly agree that I am implementing" and "I agree that I am implementing" say the same thing. Either I am or I am not.

The *strongly agree* to *strongly disagree* scale is an intensity scale; yet the item calls for an answer indicating an amount or how much.

Note that when an "amount" scale is used, it makes the item capable of being answered. Now when asked my degree of implementation, I can respond from *fully* to *partially* to *not implemented*.

9. When using a scale for answer alternatives, try to create equal intervals between adjacent choices, both semantically and spatially.

NOT:	strongly agree	mostly agree	mostly disagree	strongly disagree

INSTEAD:	strongly agree	agree	slightly agree	slightly disagree	disagree	strongly disagree

"Equal semantic distance" among the choices means that when we read the words from left to right, we want the distances between the descriptions to *feel* about the same. In the first scale above, the distance between *strongly agree* and *mostly agree* is very small. Then from *mostly agree* to *mostly disagree*, the distance is quite large. The distance between the final two choices becomes very small again. The second example is better because it gives the respondent more choices and has approximately equal intervals. Sometimes it is difficult to create intervals that have equal semantic distance. In that case, a scale with labeling only at the two endpoints is acceptable. It would look like this:

not at all   to a great degree

| 1 | 2 | 3 | 4 | 5 | 6 |

"Equal intervals" also applies to spatial distance, the measurable physical space between and among choices on a scale. Though it may seem obvious, carelessness can result in a product where choices are not separated by equal space resulting in a perception of inequity among choices (Dillman, 2007). Suffice to say, space your choices at equal intervals from one another. Web-based survey software does this automatically. Typically, your only task is to select vertical or horizontal alignment and label the choices appropriately.

10. We prefer neutral responses such as *not sure* or *undecided* be kept off the scale or, if included, to be separated spatially from the other choices. Some researchers question whether these responses are actually part of an "intensity" scale; they are certainly not part of an "amount" scale. Therefore, the propriety of calculating them into arithmetic means is doubtful. According to a 1996 study by Willits and Janota (cited in Dillman, 2000), placement of the

neutral point makes a difference. Fewer respondents selected the neutral option when it was at the end of the scale. The following example illustrates the recommended placement.

Rather than

strongly agree	agree	not sure	disagree	strongly disagree
5	4	3	2	1

consider something like

strongly agree	agree	disagree	strongly disagree	not sure
4	3	2	1	☐

One could argue in the first case that *not sure* is part of the scale and that an average of 3.4 lies somewhere between *not sure* and *agree,* but we maintain that on the 4-point scale, an average of 2.4 has more meaning (if you choose to calculate averages).

11. Avoid using absolutes such as *all* or *none, always* or *never.* These words cause problems when they are part of the question stem and when used as end-points on a scale. In the example that follows, note the problem in the stem. With a scale as a response format, placing these absolute terms at the two ends of the scale restricts the respondents' choices because many will not select an absolute.

    NOT (on a *strongly agree* to *strongly disagree* scale): *All students should be encouraged to participate in extracurricular activities.*

    INSTEAD (on a *strongly agree* to *strongly disagree* scale): *Students should be encouraged to participate in extracurricular activities.*

A respondent may strongly favor extracurricular participation. However, there may be instances when it would not be a good idea for a student to participate. In this case, the word *all* forces this person to disagree, a response that does not reflect his or her actual position.

Absolutes, such as *always* at one end of a scale and *never* at the other end will deter one's answering at the endpoints. If a respondent answers accurately, rarely will either of these two choices be correct. For example, "How often do you exercise at least three times a week?" is a question asked of a group of teachers. Even the most committed will not be able to answer *always* honestly.

12. Avoid using two qualifiers. Place a qualifier in the stem or the response, not both.

> NOT (on a *strongly agree* to *strongly disagree* scale): *The principal is usually available.*

> INSTEAD (on a *strongly agree* to *strongly disagree* scale): *The principal is available.*

The word *usually* is a qualifier, as is *strongly*. You may strongly agree that the principal is available or agree that he or she is usually available. But to strongly agree that the principal is usually available is not very meaningful.

> NOT (on a *definitely yes* to *definitely no* scale): *Do you believe you have adequate opportunities to gain the skills you need to implement the mathematics program?*

> INSTEAD (on a *definitely yes* to *definitely no* scale): *Do you believe you have the opportunity to gain skills you need to implement the mathematics program?*
> *Adequate* is a qualifier. *Definite* is a qualifier. When I say I definitely have adequate opportunity, what am I saying? Either I definitely have opportunities, or I have adequate opportunities.

GUARD AGAINST A RESPONSE SET

Avoid phrasing items in a manner that may foster a "response set." A response set is a condition of mind that causes a respondent to answer each specific question according to a conscious or unconscious bias. For example, if a respondent thinks a certain education program is terrible, he or she may give an unfavorable response to each question related to that program without really reading the items. Here are two ways to guard against a response set:

1. Describe in the directions what a possible response set is; tell the respondents that they could fall victim to their own unconscious bias and ask them to make a conscious effort to avoid doing so. Ask them to consider each item on its own merit.

2. Do not word all items in the same direction. Vary questions so that opinions will be reflected by positive responses in some instances and negative responses in others. Assume that you are critical of the current reading program for the primary grades because it does not adequately meet the needs of low achievers, and you would like to see it changed. You and other primary teachers in the district are asked to complete a questionnaire asking your feelings about the program. Note the following two questions. If you dislike the program you would answer "yes" to the first question, but you would answer "no" to the second. This type of questioning might be used to keep the respondents from establishing a response set and marking all "yes" or all "no," perhaps without even reading the questions.

Are you in favor of changing the current reading program in the primary grades?

Do you believe the current reading program in the primary grades adequately addresses the needs of low achievers?

This technique, and anything else you can do to vary the wording, forces a respondent to read each question. Using boldface print or italics for important words also helps focus the respondent.

CAUTION: When altering items to require both yes and no answers to represent a particular position, it is easy to create items with double negatives. Proof and edit carefully to avoid such semantic errors.

NOTE: Resource A is a checklist that reinforces the guidelines explained in Stage 3; check your items against the checklist to ensure correct and clear item writing.

4

Designing the Questionnaire

How the form looks, not what it contains, is the focus of Stage 4. The respondent's attitude toward a questionnaire is often determined at first glance by *how the form looks*, not by *what it contains* (Dillman, 2000; Thomas, 2004). Format includes not only the arrangement of various parts but particulars such as type size and style. It makes no sense to write clear, concise, clean questions only to have them crowded onto the page or printed in type too small to be easily read. The format should reflect the quality of the content. Just as graphic designers and advertisers consider elements of design, so does the astute questionnaire designer. Recommendations for length, formatting and design included in this chapter are consistent with Dillman's (2000, 2007) tailored design method, and they make sense to us.

NOTE: In general, rules of design apply equally to both paper-and-pencil and Web-based formats with some additional considerations for the latter. (See Chapter 12, "To Web or Not to Web," for specifics related to online design.)

LIMIT LENGTH OF FORM/TIME TO COMPLETE

The length of the form is important. If it is too long, the respondent may not feel like completing the whole thing, and responses to the last questions may reflect fatigue. The respondent will not continue to read as carefully after answering for a prolonged period of time. We suggest a form that takes no longer than 10 to 12 minutes to complete. There are times when a questionnaire must be longer, but 10 to 12 minutes is generally appropriate. It should be noted here that the wise selection of format options will save time for the respondent and allow the developer to obtain more information in a shorter period of time.

Questionnaire length cannot always be kept within our arbitrary 10-minute rule. For the researcher in that dilemma, other format and design elements can sometimes compensate. Chapter 9, "Marketing the Questionnaire," discusses this further.

ENSURE THAT EACH PAGE IS INDEPENDENT

If scales and response alternatives carry over from one page to the next, always reprint them on each new page. Avoid forcing respondents to refer continually to a previous page. (See Chapter 12 for Web-based application of this principle.)

LIMIT OPEN-ENDED RESPONSES

Open-ended questions, those asking for a written response, should be included as part of a questionnaire only after serious consideration. They are easy to write, but the ease of writing is countered by the difficulty of summarizing and analyzing the information. For paper-and-pencil surveys, an effective way to pose questions for open-ended answers is to allot one page of the questionnaire to this section. Identify the issues you would like respondents to address and ask for responses to two questions for each issue: For example, What positive comments do you have? What suggestions do you have for improvement? Present the section as shown in Figure 4.1 (usually in landscape). The example lists components typical of many instructional programs.

Example

Directions: What are your views regarding Program XYZ? In the space allocated below, you are invited to respond personally with positive comments and/or suggestions for improvement regarding identified components of the program. <u>Respond only for those items for which you have strong feelings; leave other spaces blank. Please keep your comments within the allotted space.</u>

Program Components	Positive Comments	Suggestions for Improvement
Instructional materials		
Benchmark assessments		
Staff development provided		
Collaboration with other teachers re: program implementation		

Figure 4.1

The advantages of using this format for open-ended questions are numerous. Immediately, you can make statements such as, *Fifty-two of the 85 respondents to the questionnaire made positive comments about the instructional materials for the program, whereas only 13 had a complimentary comment about the benchmark assessments. Regarding suggestions for improvement, only 11 teachers offered suggestions to improve some aspect of the materials; in the same column, 67 of the 85 felt the assessments needed improvement*

One of the challenges when working with open-ended comments is how to cluster and summarize the statements since typically there are no parameters for speaking your piece. With the boxed format (Figure 4.1), not only are you supplied with said parameters, but you also have a head start when clustering like responses. You know that everything written in the upper left cell will refer to instructional materials and, not only that, will speak to the positive aspects of the materials.

Current research (Dillman, 2007) confirms that the amount of space available affects how much is written, with a very limited space eliciting only a word or two. Depending on your purpose, a "word or two" may prove more useful and be more easily interpreted than a paragraph, and it takes the respondent far less time to provide it.

SPACING AND USE OF WHITE SPACE

Concern for space and our awareness that perception of length can affect response rate sometimes results in an overcrowded and unattractive design. Instead of trying to fill up a page, use white space purposefully. "White space" is a strong element in design and results from both internal spacing (spacing that separates items and sections) and external spacing (margins, centering, etc.). Within each section, spacing should be more condensed with white space used to emphasize the end of one section and the beginning of another.

GROUP ITEMS WITH THE SAME FORMAT TOGETHER

Items calling for the same method of response—for example, same-scaled items or single-response items—should be grouped together. Mixing response formats within a single section requires the respondents to "switch gears" and can be confusing. In contrast, when like items are grouped together and the beginning of a new set of items is clearly presented, the respondent anticipates a new set of directions and is less apt to become frustrated. The judicious use of shading can also be used to visually separate items or sections without consuming additional space.

SELECT TYPE STYLE

Choose a type size and style that is easy to read. Ordinarily, the type size should not be smaller than 10-point (we like 12-point). Variations in font size and style should be purposeful—for example, to group items or draw attention appropriately.

Note the two examples in Figure 4.2 (page 21). The one on the left sends one message (exaggeration to the point of absurdity intended); the other sends another. The example on the left illustrates the result of inconsistent spacing and the mix of item types that forces the respondents to switch gears as they try to answer. The example on the right, on the other hand, groups like items according to type (Part 1 and Part 2) and emphasizes the separate sections with spacing and selective shading. Note also that the font style variations in Example 1 potentially introduce an element of bias, implying not too subtly the preferred answers.

LINE UP ITEMS AND RESPONSE SPACES

When horizontally providing alternatives for a respondent to check, be sure <u>that plenty of space is provided between the choices.</u> Note below, it would be easy to check in the wrong space in the first example; not so in the second.

How many minutes of "free reading" do your students get in a typical school week?
Ex. 1___less than 15___15–30 ___31–45 ___46–60___ more than 60
Ex. 2 ____less than 15 ____15–30 ____31–45 ____46–60 ____more than 60

EXERCISE PATIENCE

Plan on making revisions. It is impossible to get the whole thing right the first time through. We have constructed hundreds of questionnaires, and the average number of revisions is still three. Five is not unusual. This does not mean starting from scratch five times. But it does mean that the questionnaire experiences five iterations before saying, "We're done!"

DARE TO BE DIFFERENT

Finally, do not be afraid to try a unique approach. Respondents may pay closer attention to a questionnaire that does not look like "all the others." Part of the validation stage (to be discussed later in this book) includes trying out the questionnaire on a few people before distributing it. You'll find out then if your "unique" form is workable as well as eye-catching. What do we mean by *unique?* Here is an example of one that has worked well for us, but the directions must explain it.

Do you like coming to this school?

YES!   Yes   yes   no   No   NO!

Example 1
NOT

Example 2
INSTEAD

How important do you believe parent participation is to the success of this new program?

____ *very* ____ *somewhat* ____ *not too*

2. Would you be **willing to make personal phone** calls to our parents to encourage their participation in our new program?

____ *yes* ____ *no*

3. Do you agree or disagree **(and how much)** with the following statement: **"Generally speaking, our parents believe that their child's education is important."**

____ *strongly agree* ____ *agree* ____ *disagree* ____ *strongly disagree*

4. *How interested would you be* in making personal phone calls to our parents to encourage their participation in our new program?

____ *very* ____ *somewhat* ____ *not too*

5. How many of *your parents* helped at the school carnival?

_____

6. How many different parents visited your classroom within the past month (to observe or to help)?

_____ none _____ 1–4 _____ 4–10

_____ **more than 10**

7. Do you believe that the ***"Reading For Fun"*** night should be continued?

___ **Yes,** and keep it just the same

___ **Yes,** but it needs some changes if it is to succeed

___ **I'm not sure;** it was so much work for the benefit we got from it.

Part 1: Using the scale below, **express your opinion** by circling the number associated with your choice.

1 = *very*   2 = *somewhat*   3 = *not too*

1. How important do you believe parent participation is to the success of this new program?

1   2   3

2. How interested would you be in making personal phone calls to our parents to encourage their participation in our new program?

1   2   3

3. How important do you believe our parents are (generally speaking) to their child's school success?

1   2   3

Part 2: Below are some questions that ask for the number of parents who were involved in your classroom or participated in various activities or school functions.

Using your classroom logs, please place the number in the blanks provided. If you do not know, put DK in the blank.

No. of parents who . . .

_____ Visited your classroom during the school day (to observe or to help) during the past month

_____ Helped at the school carnival

_____ Attended our school's Back to School Night

_____ Attended the last PTA meeting

_____ Attended the "Reading For Fun" night with their child

Figure 4.2

5

Writing Directions

To the writer who has given birth to every word in a perfect questionnaire and given loving care to every element of the extremely logical format, directions may seem superfluous. *Wrong!* An otherwise flawless questionnaire can be irreparably damaged by poor or incomplete directions. Remember, once a questionnaire is distributed, any errors in it are there to stay. Again, poor directions are among those errors that, once the questionnaire has been distributed, cannot be corrected.

Simple, specific, complete instructions are a must, because even the best among us are sometimes confused by forms. Good directions help ensure that

- Respondents will find the questionnaire easy to complete (thereby increasing the chances of its return to you)
- Replies will not be invalidated because some respondents misunderstand how to complete a given section

When writing directions, remember the following rules:

1. *Make no assumptions.* Do not assume that the respondents understand what they are to do. Simply writing "Complete the following" is not enough.

2. *Keep it simple.* Be thorough and use very simple language. Note the potential problem in the following example:

   Below is a list of recognized leadership skills. How important do you believe each skill is for the principal of this school? Place a check in the column that comes closest to your feelings.

Look at the above set of directions carefully. The author has used the verb "*is*" in the second sentence. Unfortunately, in this context *is* can mean three different things:

a. *Is* might mean the respondent's personal value judgment, how important the respondent believes a skill is.

b. *Is* might be interpreted as asking the respondent to get into the head of the principal to assess how important the principal believes the skill is.

c. *Is* might mean an assessment of the principal's actual behavior. Personal value judgment, guessing as to the principal's beliefs, and the principal's actual behavior are three very different issues.

Therefore, the item was changed to read:

Below is a list of recognized leadership skills. How important do you believe each skill should be for the principal of this school? Place a check in the column that comes closest to your feelings.

3. *Emphasize.* Use underlining, capitalization, boldface, italics, and other similar techniques to emphasize important points in the directions, but don't overdo it. Including too many emphasizing points reduces the probability that the real issue will be noted.

4. *Write new directions.* As a rule, supply a new set of directions for each format change in the questionnaire. Identify sections as Part 1, Section B, and so on so that the respondent can easily find any section mentioned in the directions.

5. *Stress the need for honest responses.* It is not at all unusual for a respondent to give a socially acceptable reply on a questionnaire rather than the response most relevant to his or her own situation. We have all done it—usually without even realizing it. Often, these are items in which a particular answer indicts the respondent for not performing to expectation or reveals a value other than mainstream (e.g., *How many of the five language arts components have you implemented in your classroom? Do you believe it is possible to close the achievement gap between our more affluent and less affluent students?*) In situations such as this, one cannot depend on good directions alone to result in accurate responses. Even when respondents understand every question and the method of completion, their replies will be accurate only if they are honest. Therefore, it becomes important to stress the need for "what actually is," not "what I think should be" (see "Guard Against a Response Set," in Chapter 3).

6. *Build trust.* A guarantee of complete anonymity for the respondent encourages trust and an atmosphere that will result in an honest response. Usually no name is required on the form. For particular questionnaire sections, it may be appropriate to include a statement such as the following in the directions: "Naturally, your opinions will agree with those of some people and disagree with those of others. Please don't think about that now. Your anonymity is guaranteed. Please answer as you really feel."

There are situations, however, in which the researcher desires personal follow-up to increase the rate of response. Although anonymity is not possible in these instances, the alternative is to guarantee confidentiality. Confidentiality is when I know who you are but will reveal nothing of what you say to anyone. CAUTION: Too much explanation regarding confidentiality may raise unnecessary levels of concern (Dillman, 2000, 2007).

7. *It's not over 'til it's over.* The last direction in a questionnaire should tell the respondent what to do with the completed form, to whom it should be delivered, and any other special procedures (e.g., if it should be folded a certain way). Finally, a statement such as the following is a good way to close:

> *Thank you for your time. Please place the completed form in the enclosed stamped, self-addressed envelope and mail it.*

Samples of written directions and a variety of questionnaire formats are supplied in Resource C.

6

Who Said What?

Categorizing Respondents

Picture yourself with a stack of 200 answered questionnaires, with an important part of your study being to compare responses of teachers to principals. However, with those 200, you have no idea who (teacher? principal? elementary? secondary?) answered what. This lack of knowledge about the respondents obscures your data. More important, it prevents our being able to answer a guiding question. Again, this is an error that, at this point, cannot be corrected; in the case of something as significant as dissertation research, the study is in jeopardy.

Knowing about the respondents is important for two reasons.

- First, this knowledge enables the researcher to describe the respondent sample and to assess the degree to which the sample is representative of the population, according to the variables identified. The more representative the responding sample, the more credible will be any inferences made from the data.

- Second, the guiding questions often ask for subgroup information. For example, a question for our hypothetical study of principals' leadership skills requires the researcher to distinguish between the responses of elementary and secondary teachers. If there is no way to identify which responses are which, the question obviously cannot be answered.

Some time ago, we worked with a group who needed to distinguish between certificated and classified employees when surveying attitudes toward the workplace. The survey was beautifully done except for one thing: On the approximately 60 returned questionnaires, there was nothing to distinguish one group from the other. Oops! Remember, failure to identify subgroups is an error that cannot be corrected after the questionnaires are returned. Errors of this type, especially with high-stakes projects, are the worst kind.

Much is added to the quality of a study when a researcher can make statements such as

Teachers with less than 3 years of teaching experience responded . . . whereas those with more than 10 years' experience answered . . .

or

Parents with children in Grades K–2 feel . . . about the reading program, whereas those with children in Grades 4–6 feel . . .

Information about the respondents is often requested at the beginning of a questionnaire. However, we recommend that a section at the end of the questionnaire be used to identify categories of respondents. The reason is that we prefer that the content of the questionnaire be completed before the respondent places himself or herself into particular categories. While it is not likely, placing oneself into various demographic categories could affect how one answers.

Care should be taken not to overload this section. Include only those variables that are deemed significant. Remember, you are asking for personal information, and because you have guaranteed anonymity, or at least confidentiality, too many requests for personal information may cause respondents to be self-conscious and can affect answers, as well as needlessly lengthening the questionnaire.

If for some reason you must gather categorical information of a personal or controversial nature, explain why you need the information in a statement such as the following:

This information will be used only to help account for differences in opinion; there will be no attempt made to identify respondents. It will be understood if you choose not to answer these questions; however, a response will be very helpful to us in planning a better instructional program for our students.

At this point, we wish to bring to your attention an important consideration. Sometimes the ability to place a respondent into a particular group is too important to depend on one item at the end of the questionnaire. For example, to answer the Stage 1 question dealing with differing opinions between elementary and secondary teachers requires knowing this information. If the respondent inadvertently skips the item or for some reason chooses not to answer it, that questionnaire cannot be used in the analysis.

In such cases, we recommend one of two methods to identify the essential categories of respondents. The first is to color-code the questionnaires, in which case light blue ones, for example, might be sent to elementary teachers and tan ones to those at the secondary level. The second is to include a question someplace in the questionnaire (maybe even unrelated to the Stage 1 questions) with which respondents unobtrusively identify their category. For example,

Two items, A and B, are presented below. Elementary teachers answer item A. and secondary teachers answer item B. Do not answer the alternate item.

NOTE: For Web-based surveys, a "skip response," such as that described above, can be done automatically. See advantages of Web-based surveys in Chapter 12, "To Web or Not to Web."

MODELING THE PROCESS OF QUESTIONNAIRE DEVELOPMENT

Considering what has been presented up to this point, Stages 1, 2, 3, 4, 5, and 6, the first draft of the questionnaire dealing with principals' leadership skills is shown below. But watch out! **We purposely have made two or three errors in this draft**, *which are debriefed and corrected in the next chapter, Stage 7. We believe, however, that the items and format are worthy of modeling.*

SCHOOL PRINCIPALS' LEADERSHIP SKILLS

(This is what I observe. This is what I believe.)

The role of a school principal is very challenging today. These educators are being asked to assume greater responsibility than perhaps ever before. They are accountable for meeting a variety of local, state, and federal mandates, and the quality of student outcomes has been placed squarely on their shoulders. Our school district recognizes this and has embarked upon what will hopefully be a principals' professional development program that is "second to none." This is not a remedial, catch-up training program but rather a cutting edge, state-of-the-art effort to build the best leadership team possible.

One of the first steps in developing such a program is to assess what teachers believe are our current needs. It is important to understand that THIS IS NOT AN EVALUATION ACTIVITY. NO QUESTIONNAIRE WILL BE CONNECTED TO A PRINCIPAL. ALL RESPONSES WILL BE COMBINED TO PRESENT A PICTURE TO PROGRAM PLANNERS.

Your responses are anonymous. No one will be able to connect your questionnaire to you personally. Your honest answers are very much appreciated.

Part 1 Directions: *Following are the leadership skills that will be used to develop the program. Read each one and indicate on the 4-point scale <u>the level of performance of your current principal.</u> Place that number in the blanks provided. If you do not know or do not wish to express an opinion, <u>place an "N" in the blank. Remember! This is not an evaluation.</u>*

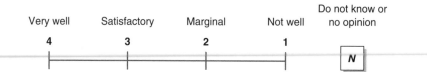

Very well	Satisfactory	Marginal	Not well	Do not know or no opinion
4	3	2	1	N

Rating

1. _____ *Establishes and communicates a vision for the organization*

2. _____ *Plans effectively for implementing school programs*

3. _____ *Demonstrates effective oral communication skills*

4. _____ *Communicates effectively with others in writing*

5. _____ *Establishes positive rapport with teachers*

6. _____ *Maintains strong relationships with parents*

7. _____ *Maintains positive rapport with students*

8. _____ *Mediates disagreements effectively*

9. _____ *Uses exemplary processes for the supervision and evaluation of instructional staff*

10. _____ *Monitors the implementation of instructional programs effectively*

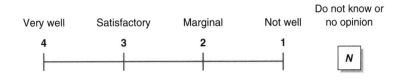

Rating

11. _____ *Promotes and guides the use of technology by school staff*

12. _____ *Solves problems effectively*

13. _____ *Promotes and supports collaborative processes*

14. _____ *Delegates and gives clear authority to complete tasks in a timely manner*

15. _____ *Ensures a positive environment for teaching and learning*

Part 2 Directions: *Considering how important you believe each skill to be to the over-all success of your school, along with the current performance level of your principal, <u>which five would you concentrate on first</u> when developing the leadership training program? When finished, you will have five check marks in the blanks.*

WHICH FIVE FIRST?

1. _____ *Establishes and communicates a vision for the organization*

2. _____ *Plans effectively for implementing school programs*

3. _____ *Demonstrates effective oral communication skills*

4. _____ *Communicates effectively with others in writing*

5. _____ *Establishes positive rapport with teachers*

6. _____ *Maintains strong relationships with parents*

7. _____ *Maintains positive rapport with students*

8. _____ *Mediates disagreements effectively*

9. _____ *Uses exemplary processes for the supervision and evaluation of instructional staff*

10. _____ *Monitors the implementation of instructional programs effectively*

11. _____ *Promotes and guides the use of technology by school staff*

12. _____ *Solves problems effectively*

13. _____ *Promotes and supports collaborative processes*

14. _____ *Delegates and gives clear authority to complete tasks in a timely manner*

15. _____ *Ensures a positive environment for teaching and learning*

Part 3 Directions: *Please supply the following information by checking the spaces that apply to you. This information will be used only to assist in planning for the leadership development program and to enable us to describe our group of respondents.*

1. Number of years at this school
   _____ 1–2
   _____ 3–5
   _____ 6–10
   _____ more than 10

2. Your gender
   _____ Female
   _____ Male

Thank you very much for your time. Place your completed form in the envelope provided, seal it, and return it to the locked mail box in the main office.

7

Conducting the Alignment Check

After the first draft of your questionnaire has been completed, a critically important step comes next: cross-referencing the proposed questionnaire items with the Stage 1 questions, including your Stage 2 operational definitions. We cannot overemphasize the importance of answering the following question: *Will the guiding questions in Stage 1 be answered by the questionnaire?* The Venn diagram in Figure 7.1 shows this intent. Potentially, if the circle on the left represents Stage 1 questions and the circle on the right the proposed questionnaire items, three different situations could result. Area 1 represents Stage 1 questions (or parts of questions) that cannot be answered by the questionnaire. Area 3, on the other hand, identifies superfluous questionnaire items. Only Area 2 represents items that are essential. The goal, of course, is for the two circles to become one—a perfect match.

The alignment check is an especially important stage for the inexperienced questionnaire developer. Although we have consulted with businesses, school districts, and graduate students, we have yet to see a first draft of a questionnaire in which this perfect match was accomplished.

Consider what the result will be if this step is not carefully carried out. If Area 1 is not discovered and the questionnaire is sent out, the result will be incomplete, leading to frustration. It will be impossible to answer all the guiding questions proposed

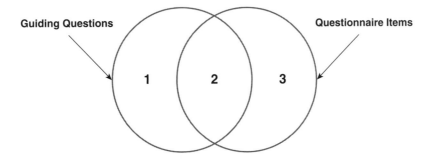

Figure 7.1   Cross-Referencing Guiding Questions With Questionnaire Items

during Stages 1 and 2. Once the questionnaire has been distributed, this error cannot be corrected. In other words, this high-stakes activity, whether it is a program evaluation or a dissertation, is in jeopardy from the start. Failure to attend to Area 3 results in a questionnaire that is longer than it needs to be, with a probable reduction in the rate of return and a higher risk of inaccurate responses due to fatigue.

A recommended alignment procedure is to create a matrix in which the questions to be answered (Stage 1 guiding questions) occupy one dimension and the questionnaire items the other. Simply go through each item and check which of the guiding questions each item refers to.

Figure 7.2 exemplifies the result of the alignment process. The alignment matrix identifies the errors and omissions clearly. Notice that the researcher will be unable to answer Question C and that questionnaire Items 2, 5, 8, 11, 14, and 15 are unnecessary.

Questionnaire Items

	1	2	3	4	5	6	7	8	9	10	11	12	13	14	15
Stage 1 Question A	X	X	X			X									
Stage 1 Question B						X	X		X	X		X	X		
Stage 1 Question C															

Figure 7.2   Sample Alignment Check

MODELING THE PROCESS

The guiding questions from the leadership skills example posed in Stage 1 are repeated below:

1. *What are the perceptions of our teachers relative to principals' performance on a selected set of leadership skills?*

2. *Are there differences in responses according to (a) school level (elementary or secondary) or (b) years at the same school?*

3. *Of the skills listed, which do teachers believe are the most important to address; that is, which skills are foundational to the new leadership training program?*

The reader will observe that Part 1 of the prototype questionnaire (pp. 30–32) relates directly to the operational definition of the term "leadership skills," with 15 items included. These 15 items were in Part I of the questionnaire because of the operational definition of "leadership skills."

Part 2 of the questionnaire dealt with the importance of the skills, and Part 3 asked some identifying information. **Red Flag Alert!** *Look carefully at Part 3 of the questionnaire. You will see that the second Stage 1 question, comparing elementary to secondary responses, cannot be answered. The first and third can, but the second cannot. Had this questionnaire been distributed without the alignment check and elementary and secondary differences were to have been an important part of the study, the researcher would have been out of luck.*

Section 3 was revised and appears as follows:

Part 3 Directions: *Please supply the following information by checking the spaces that apply to you. This information will be used only to assist in planning for the leadership development program and to describe the characteristics of our respondents.*

1. *Number of years at this school*
   ___ *1–2*
   ___ *3–5*
   ___ *6–10*
   ___ *more than 10*

2. *Your school level*
   ___ *Elementary (K–6)*
   ___ *Secondary (7–12)*

3. *Gender*
   ___ *Female*
   ___ *Male*

As illustrated above, conducting an alignment check provides a safety net for the novice researcher. Lack of alignment can result in omissions in data, as well as the collection of unneeded information. **Resource A presents a checklist to self-assess the quality of your questionnaire. Each of the "do's" and "don'ts" discussed in Chapters 1 through 7 are included in this simple tool. The list may be copied and used as a positive support to your work before you move to Stage 8, validating your instrument.**

8

Instrument Validity and Reliability

Obviously, when we collect data of any kind, we want the data to reflect what is true. We want confidence in the data's accuracy, and we want readers to give credibility to reported findings. It follows, if we are to realize these objectives, that the instruments used to collect the data must be good. "Good" in this context means that (a) the instrument must address the intended content as defined in Stages 1 and 2, (b) the instrument must elicit accurate information, and (c) the instrument must measure consistently (i.e., what a respondent says now and what he or she says a week from now should be the same thing, assuming there is no altering intervention).

Before data collection occurs via a questionnaire or some other tool, we need to be confident that the instrument is capable of meeting the three criteria listed above. Therefore, after developing a questionnaire, but before administering it, researchers (and school personnel responsible for survey activity) validate the instrument. That is, they proceed through a series of steps to answer these questions:

1. Does the instrument address the intended content?

2. Does the instrument elicit accurate information?

3. Does the instrument measure consistently over time (i.e., is the instrument reliable and trustworthy?)

This chapter describes how a researcher or a local educator can answer these questions with relative simplicity, meaning without academic training in measurement and statistics.

This stage of questionnaire development should be taken very seriously. On many occasions, the reason for educational surveying is to assist in decision making related to school improvement issues, local policy, curriculum selections, and the like. A poor instrument will produce inaccurate information, easily resulting in faulty decision making.

DOES THE INSTRUMENT ADDRESS THE INTENDED CONTENT?

If the instrument addresses the intended content, it has "content validity." Assume that a questionnaire asks school principals about their role in implementing a standards-based math program. Possible activities are listed, and the principals select those that describe what they do at their schools. Are the items on the list the most appropriate ones? Do they reflect the elements of leading a school in implementing standards-based math? Have any important elements been overlooked?

Or as in an earlier example, if we are measuring students' attitudes toward school, are the descriptors in the questionnaire appropriate, clear, and relatively complete?

The preceding two paragraphs should strike a familiar note with Stage 2, Operationalizing the Stage 1 guiding questions. If Stage 2 was done well, the probability of claiming content validity will be increased.

To establish content validity, the researcher cross-references the content of the instrument to those elements reported in the literature and supported by experience—and determines whether there is a match. In addition, the researcher asks a group of four or five specialists in the area to review the instrument and agree that "Yes, these are the appropriate items to get at what is desired." At the same time, of course, these specialists can offer suggestions regarding additions or deletions to enhance the content validity of the instrument.

If Stage 7, the Alignment Check, was done well, it is almost a guarantee that content validity has been addressed.

DOES THE INSTRUMENT ELICIT ACCURATE INFORMATION?

In other words, will the instrument discriminate among those who actually do a particular thing or feel a particular way and those who do not? If they do not, then there is a problem with our instrument and revision is in order. Inaccuracy in responses typically arises from one of two causes: (1) The instrument is poorly constructed, and/or (2) the questions address highly sensitive issues, and respondents are hesitant to respond honestly.

Poor Instrument Construction

If an instrument is poorly constructed, if it includes unclear directions, complex response formats, vague phrases, words that respondents do not understand, and so on, the likelihood of obtaining accurate information is virtually zero. Resource A provides a checklist to self-assess the quality of a newly developed tool. In addition to checking it yourself, give the questionnaire and the checklist to a few qualified people and ask them for a very frank assessment. The checklist from Resource A will help guide reviewers through the instrument—as opposed to, "Will you read this over and see if it's okay?"

Dealing With Sensitive Topics

Sensitive topics are those that can cause participants to respond less than honestly. Some issues include a degree of "social pressure" that may motivate a less than truthful response. In Chapter 3, we address this issue in terms of item construction. Here, we discuss it further as an issue of validity. In other words, we want to ensure that we are successful in eliciting honest answers. To expand upon this, let us revisit one of the examples posed in the content validity discussion above: school principals' roles in implementing standards-based instruction.

If a researcher wants to know what activities principals have engaged in with respect to standards-based instruction and includes such items on the questionnaire, how does the researcher know the principals' answers are accurate? If a principal is not doing anything in this area, will the instrument elicit such a response? Or because standards-based instruction is currently considered "the thing to do," might principals say they are doing something when really they are not? Of course, we never will know for certain, but we can consciously guard against respondents giving socially desirable answers by carefully wording the items—and the directions.

In the case of this example, we are interested in the ability of the instrument to discriminate between doers and nondoers. To this end, select a pilot group of three or four principals who are known to fit the established criteria of involvement in standards-based instruction and three or four who are not. *If possible, none of these principals would be a part of the actual study.*

Administer the instrument to the "pilot principals," keeping track of who completes the form (e.g., give doers the tan ones and nondoers the green ones). Carefully analyze how the principals respond. Study the extent to which each principal responds as you hoped he or she would, based on your prior knowledge. If the results are unacceptable (i.e., there is no real difference between the two groups), then revision of the instrument is in order and a second pilot will be necessary—perhaps not to the same group but to a group whose members fit the same doer/nondoer pattern.

Here is an important point to remember: If the instrument is not capable of discriminating, we must assume the problem lies with the instrument and not with the individuals completing the form (although, of course, that is arguable). Though we try as hard as we can and revise and revise and revise, the tendency to self-report in a way that makes us look good is part of the problem with any questionnaire and is always a limitation of any study in which it is important to sort feelings, opinions, or actions.

DOES THE INSTRUMENT MEASURE CONSISTENTLY OVER TIME?

Is the instrument reliable? Trustworthy? Have you ever completed a questionnaire, sent it back, and then said to yourself, "If I filled this out again, I'd probably say something different"? An important challenge for the developer is to design an instrument that will elicit consistent (close to the same) responses over time, assuming no intervention. This is called "reliability."

To establish the reliability of an instrument (without a statistical thought in your head), select a reliability sample, a group of 15 or so individuals who will not be a part of your study but who are thought to belong to the same category or categories of respondents as those in the study (e.g., elementary principals or members of boards of education). This match may not always be possible, but try. Administer the instrument to the group and then, a few days later, administer it again to the same group. This must be managed in such a way that the researcher can match each individual's first administration with the second. Some means, such as providing the last four digits of the Social Security number on both administrations, would be established. Incidentally, you are asking a lot of this group, so they deserve some measure of appreciation (e.g., a gift, a small remuneration). And of course they know, up front, that completion of two instruments will be necessary. One additional point: *The individuals in the reliability sample should be cautioned against trying to remember what they answered on the first administration. Ask them to answer as they currently feel.*

Subjective (Nonstatistical) Method for Establishing Reliability Item by Item

When you have two complete sets of responses from the reliability sample as described above, match each person's first and second response on each item. Do respondents say the same thing or close to the same thing? When using scales such as 1 to 6, how many of the ratings were the same? How many were off by one (1)? Though we know of no cited resource for what your reliability standard should be, experience suggests to us that at least 70% of the responses for any item should be the same and fewer than 5% should be off by more than one (1). If an item does not meet this standard, revision may be in order. Typically, when a few items do not make it and most of the others do, careful review of the problematic items usually shows why. Note that the 70% is an arbitrary standard and can be adjusted, but the 5% "off by more than 1" should not be compromised. Yes, there are always extenuating circumstances. However, if "agree" is one scale choice different from "disagree" on a 4-point scale, it would count as "off by more than 1." Evaluate each item on its own merits.

<u>Scenario:</u> *Here are the results obtained for four items after 15 teachers completed a questionnaire twice. (Remember that this example tests responses to scaled items: "off by 1" means one scale choice different—e.g. "strongly agree" during the initial administration and "agree" during the second.)*

Item	Same Response	Off by 1	Off by More Than 1
1	13	2	0
2	9	2	4
3	12	2	0
4	7	6	2

Consider Items 1 and 3 to be reliable, whereas Items 2 and 4 are questionable, suggesting a need for revision or deletion. Seventy percent of the 15 teachers is about 11 and 5% of 15 is close to 1. Even if we were a bit liberal with our self-imposed standard, far too few of

Item 4 responses were the same, and considerably more than one of the Item 2 responses were off by more than 1 rating.

AND FINALLY, YOU ASK: "DO I REALLY NEED TO DO ALL THIS?"

We have tried to convince you in the first third of this book that there are aspects of questionnaire development that appear simple to do yet can really pull the quality of the instrument down if not attended to. From the Stage 1 guiding questions to writing directions and categorizing respondents, slipups abound for all of us. If the questionnaire is a part of a high-stakes research project (e.g., significant decisions to be made regarding educational issues; a dissertation that needs to be as close to flawless as possible), then, yes, this is necessary. You must have credible findings. It's nonnegotiable.

When an instrument is validated appropriately, much will have been accomplished toward producing credible findings. A researcher who wishes to avoid the "garbage in, garbage out" syndrome will approach this aspect of a research endeavor with great care. Validity and reliability methodology is typically included in Chapter 3 of the graduate student's thesis.

9

Marketing the Questionnaire

Ensuring Response

Unfortunately, even when one has written the world's best questionnaire, there is no guarantee that it will result in enough response to give a meaningful stockpile of data. For this reason, the least technical part of the document becomes one of the most important: *marketing the questionnaire to those we hope will respond.* As stated by Dillman (2000), the "relationship between length and response rate is likely to decrease when one uses more response-inducing techniques" (p. 306). Regardless of the length of your instrument, understanding and using as many "response-inducing" techniques as possible will improve the chances for a high response rate.

To help ensure an adequate response, the marketing strategy must "sell" the potential respondent on completing and returning the form, yet do so in a way that avoids biasing the respondent and that preserves the integrity of the process. Although there are instances of mandatory participation, we assume here that you, as typically occurs in educational settings, are counting on voluntary participation. The reality is that although the questionnaire appears short and irresistible to you, it may seem burdensome to your would-be participants. Effective marketing requires a convincing and creative approach that explains the importance and usefulness of responding to a harried administrator, teacher, district office staff person, parent, or community member who may see it as just another long, boring form.

Marketing begins with the design of the questionnaire, accelerates with prenotification, and concludes with the final follow-up reminder. Marketing does not end until the last response is received. Each of these three elements of design—how you introduce the activity to respondents, including prenotification, and following up with reminders—increases the odds for a good return rate. A fourth area for consideration is the use of incentives.

43

DESIGN ELEMENTS THAT INVITE RESPONSE

In Stages 3 and 4, "Writing Items and Formatting Responses" and "Designing the Questionnaire," we pointed out the significance of an attractive questionnaire. We addressed elements of spacing, the importance of white space, and overall appearance. We urged clustering of like items and the purposeful use of font size and style to separate sections and to emphasize important issues. We also suggested that a shorter questionnaire is more inviting than a longer instrument. First impressions DO make a difference. The title of your questionnaire and the nature of Question 1 can either encourage, or discourage, response.

Title

We suggest avoiding the word *questionnaire* in the title. For many, questionnaire connotes long and dull. Construct a title that describes the content. A clever but general title can be followed by a more formal title as in the following examples.

> A Matter of Opinion: Staff Response to Standards-Based Instruction
>
> What Are Your Thoughts? Evaluation of the Language Arts Curriculum
>
> Tell It Like It Is: Your Experience as a Parent Volunteer

Question 1

Don Dillman (2007), creator of the tailored design method for surveys who is referenced often in this text, advises that the first question is particularly important: It should apply to every respondent, be easy to answer, and invite interest. "Interest" is in the eye of the respondent. You know who you are targeting; use that knowledge to your advantage. This first item may not lie at the heart of the survey but, rather, serve as an interesting jumping-off point. Note the example below using the leadership scenario integrated throughout the book.

> 1. *Does school leadership matter? How important is the role of a school principal to the overall quality of a school? On a scale of 1 to 10, with 10 being* crucial *and 1 equaling* insignificant, *rate the importance of the principal's role. Circle the number that comes closest to your feelings.*

Insignificant   *Crucial*

  1   2   3   4   5   6   7   8   9   10

Note that the example applies to all respondents, it invites an opinion of an important issue, and the directions are clear and specific. It's a start!

INTRODUCING THE ACTIVITY TO THE RESPONDENT

Prenotification

Few of us welcome sudden requests for our time, and a request to respond to a survey is just that—a request for respondents' time. Hence, an advanced warning in the form of prenotification is important. Prenotification informs the potential respondents that "it's on the way!" with an encouraging request to "please respond" and is an effective response inducement (e.g., Dillman, 2000, 2007; Solomon, 2001; Schonlau, Fricker, & Elliott, 2002; Thomas, 2004). The more personal your prenotification, the greater the impact. A telephone call is ideal but often impractical. In lieu of a telephone call, a postcard or e-mail can suffice.

The mode of your prenotification need not be the same as your survey administration. A phone call may be used to introduce an electronic survey, or an e-mail sent to notify potential respondents that a survey is in the mail. The intent is to ensure that the arrival of a questionnaire is not a surprise. At best, a prenotification is brief, clear, and enticing. Building on our school leadership scenario, the following is offered as an example.

Your opinion, please! In a week to 10 days, you, and every teacher in our district will receive, via mail, a brief questionnaire focusing on the leadership skills required of today's school principals. Results of this survey will have an impact on our district's future, and we are hoping for a 100% response. Please be on the alert for this very important document. Thank you in advance for this gift of time.

Sincerely,

District X Leadership Team (names of team members add credibility to this request)

Introductory Letter

A compelling letter of introduction should accompany a mailed questionnaire. The following items should be included:

- A brief introduction
- Purpose of the form
- Why the recipient's response is important
- How long it will take to complete the form
- When and how the respondent will be informed of the results
- A guarantee of confidentiality (if this might be an issue)

If the introduction is short, to the point, and intriguing, the recipient will anticipate the same qualities in the questionnaire that follows. Assure the recipient of the questionnaire's importance by printing the introduction as a cover letter on appropriate letterhead, signed by you, and if possible, a person with whom the respondents will identify. Endorsements by someone familiar to the respondents add to the perceived "importance" of the request and support a return (Huang, Hubbard, & Mulveny, 2003). One group often not considered in the marketing effort is students. The student council president or some other student with whom potential respondents can identify can provide a recognizable signature on an introductory letter. And don't forget in an elementary school when addressing parents . . . the child's teacher. Figure 9.1 provides an example based on our school leadership scenario. See Resource B for more samples.

MODELING THE PROCESS

Consider the example of the leadership skills questionnaire. The introductory letter might look like this:

Letterhead

Date

Dear (personalized, if possible):

 Part of the unknown future is the changing role and responsibilities of the building principal. In that context, what leadership skills are needed to build a dynamic, high-quality school? Answering that question is especially important for our school district since we are growing and anticipate hiring a number of new site administrators over the next few years.

 What leadership skills and dispositions should we look for in a new principal? What skills should we nurture and support among our current leaders? How might the skills required of an elementary school principal be the same or different from those required of a secondary principal?

 Who better to answer those questions than teachers?

 Your responses will help us in the design of a professional development program for our current and future site administrators, with the intention of helping them become the best they can be!

 The enclosed form lists several leadership skills and asks your opinions about the presence or absence of each skill in your current principal. **This is not an evaluation of principals***; responses will not be associated with any individual site. Responses from across the district will be combined to present a picture of teachers' perceptions in this important area. The form takes less than 10 minutes to complete.*

 This study has the support of our principals and the teachers' association: nevertheless, the topic is a sensitive one and anonymity is guaranteed.

 Thank you for your time. You may review the summative results of this study on the District Web page, beginning _____.

Sincerely,

(Signature)

Figure 9.1 Sample Introductory Letter

DELIVERY AND RETURN

Delivery and the manner in which you request the return convey symbolic messages regarding the importance of the research and the regard you have for the response of each individual. More than one piece of research recommends a "real stamp" (Dillman, 2000). First-class postage connotes more importance than bulk rate, and a real stamp is more personal than a metered stamp; Hager, Wilson, Pollak, and Rooney (2003) reported that in a survey of nonprofit executives, Federal Express delivery as opposed to standard mail resulted in an improved response. Again, delivery mode can add to or minimize perceptions of importance. Pay attention, also, to the method of return. For a mail questionnaire, a self-addressed envelope with appropriate postage should be included as part of the package.

FOLLOW-UP REQUEST TO NONRESPONDENTS

Although your goal may be a 100% response on a mailed questionnaire, you will not get it. Nevertheless, the greater the response rate, the more credible the results. Therefore, obtaining as many returns as possible becomes an important issue. General guidelines for maximizing the impact of your follow-up contacts is the same as for prenotification: The more personal the approach, the greater the response. Regardless of whether the questionnaire is mailed, e-mailed, or Web based, a follow-up to nonrespondents in a different mode is recommended (Dillman, 2007). Your follow-up contact should be in the form of a "friendly reminder"; no one appreciates being nagged. We recommend the following specific steps:

First, about a week after the initial mailing, send a postcard that reads something like Figure 9.2. We generally experience a small increase in responses (nothing monumental) with this process.

Second, after three weeks or so, and assuming you have kept a record of who has returned and who has not, send another entire package, including a different letter and the questionnaire with the stamped envelope.

Finally, if the response rate is still too small, making personal phone calls becomes necessary.

Dear Educator,

Not long ago you received a request to respond to an inquiry about the importance of selected leadership skills for school principals. If you have returned the form, thank you very much.

If, on the other hand, you have yet to return the form, might you consider it now? Your opinions are important and will help in planning future staff development programs.

If you have misplaced the form, I would be pleased to send you another one. Call collect, 714-281-XXXX, and I will send you another one. Thanks for your consideration.

Name

Figure 9.2 Sample Follow-Up Postcard

WHAT ABOUT INCENTIVES?

Preincentives—a small monetary reward, a dollar bill, or a small gift—sent as a "token of appreciation" have become increasingly popular and for a reason: incentives are a proven response-inducing technique (e.g., Huang et al., 2003; Dillman, 2000; Schonlau et al., 2002). Perhaps you, too, have a sense of obligation when you receive something of value in advance of completing a survey. Some years ago, we included a rather generous incentive ($5 gift certificate to a bookstore) as an inducement for respondents to volunteer for follow-up contact. The response was gratifying, but one respondent, a high school teacher, took us to task for commercializing our effort. You know your audience, or should, and the consideration of incentives should include the possibility of some backlash. Intuitively, we suspect that in the field of education, incentives may not make much of an impact one way or the other.

Providing an incentive electronically requires a "modern" approach. Coupons, inclusion in a lottery, or gift certificates are doable options if you decide to go this route.

Chapter 9, "Marketing the Questionnaire," concludes the nine "stages" of questionnaire development; once that last reminder has been sent, your role changes from seeker of data to recipient. And the work has just begun. Chapters 10 and 11 provide direction on data analysis and reporting results.

Part II

Getting from Here to There

10

The Process of Data Analysis

The intended audience for this book is the inexperienced researcher/educator for whom data gathering is not a routine activity. The book focuses primarily on questionnaire development, but two additional chapters on data analysis and reporting of results are offered here to assist in the process. Although the chapters do not cover these topics in detail, they point the reader in the desired direction with some suggestions and examples. Chapter 10 addresses data analysis, and Chapter 11 discusses how to report the results of analysis.

I n the decade since the first edition of *Your Opinion, Please!* was published, the world of data analysis has changed dramatically. In 1996, this chapter included a process for hand tabulating survey responses effectively, the assumption then being that large numbers of educators in the schools did not have access to electronic data entry and processing; or if they did, they lacked the experience to use it. Eleven years later, that assumption is no longer valid, and this section now recognizes that data entry and subsequent processing are available to the vast majority of educators. Also, a decade ago, many of the computer printouts reporting questionnaire results were awkward, often producing too many pages to comfortably work with and column and row labeling (or lack of it) that prevented one from effectively and efficiently doing the work. That, too, has been resolved to a great degree. Nevertheless, there are still important suggestions and cautions that the neophyte would do well to heed.

When preparing for data analysis, there is one issue to continuously keep on the front burner: *Our most important concern is answering the guiding questions, clearly and succinctly.* Conditions, sometimes within and sometimes beyond our control, can deter attaining this goal; thus, we spend needless hours trying to stay (or get) organized in preparation for writing. Once again, we go slow to go fast.

PREPARING FOR DATA ANALYSIS

Two tasks are necessary to complete before analyzing your results: (1) entering your data into the computer and (2) designing prototype tables to display your findings. In concert with our "go slow to go fast" mantra, spending time up front to complete these tasks will pay huge dividends down the road.

Entering Your Data

Make certain that you understand the requirements of the software that you will use to produce the necessary printouts. Learning how the data are to be entered, coding of demographic information (e.g., 1 = *female*; 2 = *male*; or 1 = *one or two years of teaching experience*; 2 = *three to five years*; 3 = *six or more*), labeling variables so as to produce readable printouts, and the like are "small steps" that help guarantee getting the job done efficiently. Using an external data entry specialist accentuates the importance of attending to these issues. Remember, selecting one who is skillful at data entry may be your choice, but often these people will not understand the ins and outs of the program used to analyze the data. You must be able to clearly communicate your needs. You may also choose to employ a computer specialist to do your analysis work, but this does not relieve you of the responsibility for this initial step: labeling variables and determining appropriate coding.

The discussion that follows regarding prototype tables will also assist in planning data entry.

Designing Prototype Tables

Using your Stage 1 guiding questions as the basis for analysis preparation, we highly recommend designing and formatting the tables that you believe you will use to assist readers in answering each of the guiding questions. This is done before you receive your printout of results. Of course, at this point you will have no numbers to place in the various rows and columns, but the skeletal design will let you know what you must be able to access from the computer printouts. Furthermore, it will give you a great head start in preparing your report of findings. Note the example that follows.

Guiding Question 1 from our continuing model asked, *What are the perceptions of our teachers relative to principals' performance on a selected set of leadership skills?*

Clarifying "leadership skills" occurred during Stage 2, and among the 15 identified were these (we selected just 4 from among the 15 skills in order to keep our example simple):

1. *Establishes and communicates a vision for the organization*

2. *Plans effectively for implementing school programs*

3. *Communicates effectively with others orally*

4. *Establishes positive rapport with certificated staff members.*

The questionnaire presented the skills to the respondents and asked for a 4-point scaled response. These were *very well, satisfactory, marginal,* and *not well.* To make the table understandable, the readers will want to know how many respondents there were and how many of those answered each of the four choices. Calculating percentages of the total always helps clarify the content of a table. With this in mind, the skeletal table for these four items (will be 15 in reality) may look like Table 10.1 (the *N*s in the first column are the total number of respondents who answered an item. The small *n* is the number who gave the response to that item in that category); these letters are accepted statistical symbols to differentiate between the total number (N) and part of the total, or subgroup (n).

Table 10.1   Teachers' Perceptions of Principals' Leadership Skills on Selected Items

Skills	Very Well		Satisfactory		Marginally OK		Not Well	
	n	*%*	*n*	*%*	*n*	*%*	*n*	*%*
Establishes and communicates a vision N =								
Plans effectively for implementing programs N =								
Demonstrates effective oral communication skills N =								
Establishes positive rapport with certificated staff N =								

Two-dimensional tables with a structure similar to that shown here are very common and will serve you well when preparing for analysis and reporting. When the data have been placed into the table, the Stage 1 guiding question, *What are the perceptions of our teachers relative to principals' performance on a selected set of leadership skills?* can be answered.

The remaining two questions from the model scenario are these:

2. *Are there differences in responses according to (a) school level (elementary or secondary) or (b) years at the same school?*

3. *Of the skills listed, which do teachers believe are the most important to address; that is, which skills are foundational to the new leadership training program?*

Continuing with the above example, Sample Table 10.2 (page 53) illustrates how responses to the school level portion of Question 2 might be displayed.

Guiding Question 2: Are there differences in responses according to (a) school level (elementary or secondary) or (b) years at the same school?

Sample Table 10.2 Teachers' Responses According to School Level: Elementary or Secondary

Skills		Very Well		Satisfactory		Marginal		Not Well	
		n	*%*	*n*	*%*	*n*	*%*	*n*	*%*
Establishes and communicates a vision	Elementary N =								
	Secondary N =								
Plans effectively for implementing programs	Elementary N =								
	Secondary N =								
Demonstrates effective oral communication skills	Elementary N =								
	Secondary N =								
Establishes positive rapport with certificated staff	Elementary N =								
	Secondary N =								

The second part of Guiding Question 2 "according to years at the same school" would follow the same structure using the responses requested (1–2 years, 3–5, 6–10, more than 10). This would result in a complex table, but the complexity is necessary if we are to disaggregate as planned.

Below is a sample table for Guiding Question 3, *Of the skills listed, which do teachers believe are the most important to address; that is, which skills are foundational to the new leadership training program?* The section in the questionnaire that addressed this question presented the 15 items and asked the respondents to check the 5 that they believe should be concentrated on first when developing the leadership training program (see Chapter 6). Again, for the purposes of illustration only, the same 4 items

Sample Table 10.3   Teacher Selections of 5 Most Important Skills

Skills N =	5 Most Important	
	n	*%*
Establishes and communicates a vision		
Plans effectively for implementing programs		
Demonstrates effective oral communication skills		
Establishes positive rapport with certificated staff		

are listed, followed by the number (n) and percentage (%) who selected that item as "most important." Remember *(N)* refers to the total number of respondents.

Remember, answering Stage 1 questions is the reason the questionnaire data were collected. Each question is much more easily answered by tables similar to the above than by traipsing through pages of computer data. Planning what your tables will look like ahead of time gives you a wonderful head start.

ANALYZING YOUR DATA

When you receive your computer printout (often several pages with much unnecessary information embedded with the important data you need), we suggest that you never lose sight of our "go slow to go fast" admonishment. We suggest that before you put pencil to paper, finger to keyboard to report the results, you not skip any of these three steps: (1) understand your printout, (2) connect the printout to each guiding question, and (3) answer each guiding question. While it may seem trite on the surface, moving through these three simple steps can prevent much pain that could surface later when you suddenly realize you've read the printout incorrectly, and the figures you thought represented your findings really aren't the right ones, and the answers to your guiding questions are therefore incorrect, and the report you have just completed has the wrong information in it . . . ad nauseum.

Understand the Computer Printout

Very simply stated, with no bells and whistles, *review each page of your printout and be absolutely certain that you understand what the data say.* Refrain (if you can resist the urge) from analyzing the data. At this point, that will just get in the way of your intent. If someone else provided you with the information, go over the printout with that person. Do not, under any circumstances, leave this step until you are certain you understand what is on all those pages that you're holding in your hand.

Connect the Printout to the Guiding Questions

Computer printouts do not automatically display the answers to each guiding questions in order. While you may be able to generate data displays on the computer that approximate this, it won't typically occur. Thus, you end up with data that contribute to answering Question 1 with Question 2 with Question 4, and the like, all mixed together. While it sounds simplistic, take our advice nonetheless. Cut and paste if you must, but assemble all data relating to each guiding question in one place. Create folders labeled "Guiding Question 1," "Guiding Question 2," and the like. When the time comes to address each question analytically, every piece of information you need will be in one place.

You don't like that suggestion? Here's another way to connect data to question. Using colored highlighters, identify the data connected to each guiding question with a different color. That way you haven't mutilated your printout, yet you can identify that information related to each question. When the time comes to analytically address each question, the highlighters will lead you to the right place.

Answer Each Guiding Question

You created blank tables in which to insert the numbers once they became available. Now that you have your data, this shell (also seen on page 52) . . .

Sample Table 10.1   Teachers' Perceptions of Principals' Leadership Skills

Skills	Very Well		Satisfactory		Marginally OK		Not Well	
	n	%	n	%	n	%	n	%
Establishes and communicates a vision N =								
Plans effectively for implementing programs N =								
Demonstrates effective oral communication skills N =								
Establishes positive rapport with certificated staff N =								

. . . has now become this (an example, of course):

Sample Table 10.4   Teachers' Perceptions of Principals' Leadership Skills on Selected Items

Skills	Very Well		Satisfactory		Marginally OK		Not Well	
	n	%	n	%	n	%	n	%
Establishes and communicates a vision N = 47	10	**21**	20	**43**	11	**23**	6	**13**
Plans effectively for implementing programs N = 52	8	**15**	13	**25**	20	**38**	11	**21**
Demonstrates effective oral communication skills N = 54	10	**19**	11	**20**	13	**24**	20	**37**
Establishes positive rapport with certificated staff N = 49	25	**51**	11	**22**	6	**12**	7	**14**

For each guiding question, using the table, write a *one-paragraph answer and a summary of what the data in the table reveal*. Using minimal numbers, pretend you are giving a speech to a group of stakeholders, and the purpose is to answer those questions. What would you say? The reason for this is to place firmly in your mind the results of your study. You must be able to see the whole forest before addressing the trees. Considering only the four skills, your summary may look something like this:

Teachers' assessment of skill presence revealed that the strongest skill was establishing positive rapport with the staff, with about one-half reported to be performing "very well" and close to three-fourths in the two positive categories. Establishing and communicating a vision was also rated relatively strongly. The weaker two skills, with 6 of every 10 receiving negative ratings, dealt with planning for implementation and oral communication.

You don't like this suggestion? Then use bullets identifying the important information in the table. From these bulleted data, you will know the answer to the guiding questions. Your efforts may result in something like this:

- *Establishing rapport was the highest rated (over half "very well"; three-fourths "very well" plus "satisfactory")*

- *Two of the four had over half in the top two categories; two were less than half.*

- *The least well done was oral communication with 6 of 10 ratings in the "marginal" or "not well" categories.*

Of course, this task will be a bit more complex when all 15 skills are being considered, but clustering those skills with similar percentages to review the results will ease the task. Arranging the "very well" percentages in descending high to low order, rather than just reporting in the same order as presented in the questionnaire, will assist enormously in your understanding the results.

Before leaving our data analysis presentation, allow us to briefly discuss a very important aspect of subgroup analysis—subgroup analysis. It was briefly presented above, but only from a presentation perspective. Here, we want to extend your understanding.

THE IMPORTANCE OF ANALYZING SUBGROUP RESPONSES (DISAGGREGATING THE DATA)

We have continuously emphasized the importance of focusing on guiding questions. If a question asks, "Is there a difference of response between males and females?" or "Do college-bound students answer differently than non-college-bound students?" stunning results can sometimes occur. In fact, we would suggest that more "oh wows!" and "aha's!" will result from disaggregating data than from simply reporting results from the total group.

To illustrate, assume that a questionnaire collected information from high school students regarding various aspects of schooling, and one of the questions tried to gauge the students' overall impressions of the school by asking, "If you were to grade the quality of your school, much the same as you are given grades, what grade would you give your school?" Typical choices of A, B, C, D, or F are given. Assume further that the distribution of grades among the approximate 1,850 high school students looked like this:

Quality of My School: Responses of 1,850 High School Students

A		B		C		D		F	
N	%	N	%	N	%	N	%	N	%
463	25	520	28	673	36	104	6	97	5

You look at the data and see that about 53% of the students gave a grade of A or B, with 25% awarding the highest possible grade; about a third were in the middle, giving a C grade; and a bit above 10% gave a D or an F. In the absence of any longitudinal data or any specific standard by which to compare the results, you probably would conclude that these data are somewhat complementary. After all, there were twice as many A's as D's and F's combined.

Now look at the difference if the data are disaggregated by gender, as shown below.

Student Responses According to Gender

	A		B		C		D		F	
	N	%	N	%	N	%	N	%	N	%
Male	144	15	240	26	412	44	67	7	73	8
Female	319	35	280	30	261	28	37	4	24	3
Total	463	25	520	28	673	36	104	6	97	5

What a difference! The totals reported in the first table say one thing, and one conclusion is drawn. But when we disaggregate the data, a completely different conclusion is drawn, and a red flag goes up regarding gender differences. Just over 40% of the males gave an A or B, compared with 65% of the females. You wonder why, and you are concerned. When such dramatic differences result from disaggregating the data, they render the total numbers relatively meaningless and potentially misleading.

Additional ways to disaggregate these students' data could be by grade level or ethnicity.

Results from these groups can add greatly to the overall understanding and analysis.

11

Communicating Your Results Effectively

Three major rules or considerations must guide all aspects of effectively communicating the results of your questionnaire:

1. *Your data tell a story.* Two major elements contribute to "telling the data story." They are your tables and your narrative. The manner in which each supports the other determines the effectiveness of communication. Remember, the two are interdependent, and a weakness in either will detract significantly from the overall quality of reporting.

2. *The guiding questions,* **not** *the questionnaire, provide the basis for the narrative.* Simply put, if there are three guiding questions from Stage 1 and five questionnaire sections, the narrative should focus on the three questions, not on a step-by-step presentation of the five questionnaire sections.

3. *If you must err, err on the side of brevity.* This helps you remember that your objective is effective communication of the most important information. If you write too much, the chaff may obscure the wheat. Understandably, different audiences will require different levels of presentation (parents, general public, teachers, boards of education), but the major idea remains intact. How much you report is relative.

CREATING YOUR TABLES

Computer printouts provide the data that you will include in your tables. Remember, you will typically select only a small fraction of the information the computer provides. The following suggestions help with this task.

1. As indicated in Chapter 10, design your tables before attempting any narrative. The tables establish the foundation for the material to be highlighted in the narrative. Tables are meant to stand alone—that is, to be understandable without reading the accompanying text. When your tables are complete, ask

a critical friend to describe the tables to you; then consider how close he or she comes to your intended meaning.

2. Consider the following brief list of "be sure to's" for creating effective tables. Use the items as a checklist each time you create a table of data. Be sure to . . .

- Write table titles that report exactly what is in the table

- Label every column and every row of the table

- Avoid using too many numbers in the table

- Report group sizes (and avoid reporting percentages for small groups; e.g., < 30)

- Report whole-number percentages (reporting to tenths, or beyond, does nothing to assist understanding the content and just produces a busy table)

- Present the data in some kind of order (e.g., from high to low percentages), regardless of the order used in the questionnaire

As stated above, a key question is, "Can the tables stand alone?" Table 11.1 shows how a table can be constructed using the list of "be sure to's." The title of the table is precise, each column and row is labeled, and only whole numbers and percentages are reported. The table heading includes the total number of respondents ($N = 147$). The order presented was high to low percentages in the "Quite Desirable" column. The table can stand alone, just as it appears. Table 11.1 is a recommended display format.

Table 11.1 Elementary School Principals' Preferences Regarding Parent Participation Activities for Their Schools ($N = 147$)

Parent Activities	Quite Desirable		Somewhat Desirable		Not Sure		Not Desirable	
	N	%	N	%	N	%	N	%
Fundraising	100	68	23	16	10	7	14	10
Volunteering in the classroom or library	97	66	35	24	7	5	8	5
Serving on curriculum or instruction committees	82	56	23	16	7	5	35	24
Focusing on closer contact with businesses	80	54	45	31	20	14	2	1
Creating materials for the classroom	60	41	50	34	11	8	26	18
Tutoring other children	28	19	38	26	21	14	60	41
Monitoring the playground and cafeteria	13	9	43	29	40	27	51	35

Contrast the presentation in Table 11.1 with the one below. We went a bit over the top, but you get the idea. The reader is hard pressed to get meaning from Table 11.2, while Table 11.1 presents an immediate clear picture. Table 11.1 stands alone. Table 11.2 does not.

Table 11.2 Principals' Preferences

Activities	Quite		Somewhat		Not Sure		Not	
	N	%	N	%	N	%	N	%
Tutoring	28	19.05	38	25.85	21	14.29	60	40.82
Volunteering	97	65.99	35	23.81	7	4.76	8	5.44
Curriculum or instruction committees	82	55.78	23	15.65	7	4.76	35	23.81
Monitoring the playground and cafeteria	13	8.84	43	29.25	40	27.21	51	34.69
Fundraising	100	68.03	23	15.65	10	6.80	14	9.52
Materials for the classroom	60	40.82	50	34.01	11	7.48	26	17.69
Business contacts	80	54.42	45	30.61	20	13.60	2	1.36

WRITING THE NARRATIVE

The narrative portion of the report should focus on the guiding questions developed in Stage 1, not just on recounting how subjects responded to each section of the questionnaire. The example that follows guides the researcher by progressing through various levels of specificity in the presentation of the information shown in Table 11.1 on the previous page.

First, consider the guiding questions as subheadings for the narrative.

The guiding question that produced Table 11.1: What activities do elementary principals believe are the most desirable on their campuses to enhance ongoing parent participation?

Second, begin very generally, informing the readers about what will follow.

One hundred forty-seven elementary principals responded to seven items on the questionnaire that dealt with possible activities for parent involvement. Respondents were asked to indicate the desirability of each activity as a means of improving parent participation. Responses were on a 4-point, "quite desirable" to "undesirable," scale. Table 11.1 reports how these principals responded to the seven items.

Third, the first statements about the data presented in the table should be general. Do not start by reporting item-by-item numbers, percentages, or scores. Instead, give the reader an idea of what is to come.

Of the seven parent participation activities to which the elementary principals responded, four were deemed "quite desirable" by a majority. Of these four, only one activity involved parents in direct contact with students, whereas the other three focused on other aspects of parent involvement.

Among the seven, the activities rated most desirable clearly were those of parents assisting with fundraising and volunteering in the classroom or library. More than 65% rated these items as "quite desirable." Serving on school curriculum and instruction committees or participating in a collective effort to establish closer contact with the business community were the only other activities to be rated "quite desirable" by as many as 50% of the administrators.

Fourth, isolate particular findings or direct the reader to a portion of the table that may be particularly important.

Attention is called to the last two rows in the table. Although recommendations in the literature for enhancing parent involvement include tutoring children other than one's own and providing some form of supervision, these appear to have been soundly rejected by the group of responding principals, with fewer than 20% rating either one as highly desirable.

Also note that because a 4-point scale was used, the first two responses could be considered degrees of positive response and the last two, degrees of negative response. In examining the responses from that perspective, principals appear definite about their feelings, one way or the other. On the positive side, only two activities of the seven had higher percentages in the "somewhat desirable" than in the "quite desirable" column, and on the negative side, six of the seven had higher percentages for the more negative response.

Here are a few further pointers for helping readers understand the text:

- Be certain that all that is written has significance and will help the reader interpret the data. Do not report information in the narrative just because it happens to be in a table. Ask, "Will this piece add to the reader's understanding?"

- Never report "endless" sequences of percentages or other indices in narrative form. It is too hard to follow. How common it is to read something like, "Thirty-one percent of the respondents believe that option A is the best, with 32% favoring Option B. Option C received only 11% of the "votes," with Option D getting 19%. Option E received . . ." aargh!

- Do not report data to a higher degree of precision than is needed; the use of two or more decimal places interferes with understanding. As stated previously, we prefer whole-number percentages, both in tables and in narrative. To us, it is inconceivable that .4 or .6 is going to make any difference in making meaning from a set of data.

- Depending on the nature of your guiding questions, you may be involved with statistical tests of significance. Narrative involving these tests should be crisp and clear, communicating to the reader that you know what you are talking about. Depending on the test, simply state the results, whether significance was attained, and the meaning of the results of the statistical test.

The following examples illustrate summary comments for several frequently used tests of significance. If statistical tests of significance are not a part of your repertoire, you are invited to skip this section.

Considering differences of means:

The mean of Group A was 37.2 out of a possible 45 points; the mean for Group B was 39.6. The t test for independent samples yielded a t of 1.87, with a p value of .23. Using the .05 standard for significance, it cannot be stated that the means of the two groups are different. The probability is too great that the size of the difference may have been due to chance. Table 4 reports the results.

Considering correlations:

The correlation between Variable A and Variable B for the 47 respondents was .42, which was significant at the .01 level. This indicates that the two variables are related in that an increase in the value of one tends to be accompanied by an increase in the value of the other. The relationship, considering the variables in question, would be considered low to moderate.

Considering distributions of three groups on a 4-point continuous scale:
Because this narrative is a bit more difficult to succinctly state, a "quasi table" is provided for ease of understanding (only the essential parts of the table are included to assist).

Table 11.3

	Strong Positive	*Positive*	*Negative*	*Strong Negative*
Group A	32%			8%
Group B	11%			32%
Group C	13%			7%

Table 11.3 reports the distributions of responses on the 4-point scale for the three groups. Thirty-two percent of Group A gave a strong positive response to the issue, whereas only 11% and 13% from Groups B and C, respectively, answered similarly. Note also from Table 11.3 that slightly over 30% of Group B gave strong negative responses compared with less than 10% from Groups A and C.

REPORTING DATA FROM AN OPEN-ENDED FORMAT

When open-ended comments are requested, they generate a myriad of different responses. Your task is to take all these specific answers and cluster them so that you can report something meaningful. This is difficult to do, even for experienced data analysts. The general rule of thumb is this: *cluster and summarize.*

Suppose that a questionnaire asks for "suggestions to improve the school," followed by a priority-setting question. You will get ideas all over the board, from different textbooks for social studies to colder water in the fountains. Perhaps, after reviewing the suggestions and formally recording a sample of them, you see that they are beginning to cluster into several areas, such as communication, curriculum, pull-out programs, school safety, site maintenance, and so on. Your first step, then, is to sort all the responses into clusters. Next, you look inside each cluster to determine the kinds of suggestions being made.

In the communication cluster, for example, comments may be sorted first into "internal" and "external." That is, inside the school and outside the school. Within the internal cluster, you might further sort into categories—for example, "teachers communicating to principal" and "teachers communicating to teachers." When a clustering pattern has been established (and it can change in midstream as you continue working your way through the questionnaires), the next step is to establish a coding system. A "1" might be assigned to teacher-to-teacher communication, a "2" to teacher-to-principal communication, a "3" to school-to-parent communication, and so on. When the coding scheme has been completed, every questionnaire is then read and coded. Coding enables one to use the computer to assist in analysis.

There is a danger, however, in overly objectifying open-ended comments: You stand to lose much of the richness of the information, especially from interviews. Seek a balance, but expect to be challenged.

IMPORTANT: When comments are requested on a questionnaire, some respondents may write more than one comment; others may offer none. In your narrative or in the tables that report on comments, be sure to indicate how many individuals made comments and the total number of comments that were made. Assume, for example, that 265 principals responded to a questionnaire and one item asked for their suggestions about a particular issue. You analyze the data and prepare a narrative. In your narrative you state that "124 suggestions were made about the issue." Does this mean that 124 principals made one suggestion each, or does it mean that 59 principals made 124 suggestions? *This must be made clear.*

There is no secret potion for analyzing and reporting open-ended information—unless it is called "experience." But if you do not even try to do it well, you most assuredly will not. Your goal is to communicate, not just get the job done.

12

To Web or Not to Web

A lthough we have made brief comments regarding Web-based surveying at pertinent junctures throughout the book, little has been offered that might sway the reader one way or the other in terms of the key question: Is a Web-based survey an appropriate option for the needs of my research? It is the purpose of this section to consolidate the considerations and issues relative to Web-based versus paper-and-pencil surveying and to suggest some general criteria for making that decision. First, two caveats: We write this in the first quarter of the year 2007; ergo, some of what we present may already be behind current technology. In addition, the major thrust of *Your Opinion, Please!* is the **planning, development,** and **design** of questionnaires as well as some practical strategies for dealing with the results. Accordingly, although we include essential information regarding the logistics and other components relative to the use of the Web, development and design remain the primary focus. Throughout this book, we have used the term *Web based* or *online* to delineate electronic surveying versus paper-and-pencil surveys, without further definition. Just to clarify here, our references and discussion assume the use of a Web-based survey software program, accessible via an online provider, generally available for a one-time cost or renewable subscription.

For those of us who use e-mail daily, electronic surveying is very inviting. Among market researchers, the cost savings of Web-based technology makes it increasingly attractive (Howes & Mailloux, 2001), and the proliferation of online survey providers make the same choice available to the small-time (i.e., small-budget) researcher. On the other hand, mail-in questionnaires continue to result in a much higher response rate than do Web-based surveys; return rates for Internet surveys are lower than mail surveys (Solomon, 2001) and sometimes "abysmal" (Dillman, 2007, p. 450). These findings are not entirely consistent, however, and include some definite anomalies, such as the 2001 randomized study by Couper (cited in Schonlau, Fricker, & Elliot, 2002), which resulted in a 61% return rate by the Web responders compared with a 41% mail-in return. Rather than be discouraged or encouraged by the conflicting data, it behooves today's researcher to become informed and to make the decision "to web or not to web" based on a personal understanding of the audience, the purpose of the study, and researcher's own preference. Three areas frame this discussion: "First Things First," which examines the basic issues of respondent access, time, and cost; "Applying Design Guidelines to Web-Based Questionnaires"; and "Caveats and Cautions."

FIRST THINGS FIRST

Access

Do those in your targeted population have access to the Internet and do (will) they use it? Do your intended respondents have the necessary computer skills to navigate an online survey (Dillman, 2007; Thomas, 2004)? What kind of coverage bias will result if access is limited (Howes & Mailloux, 2001; Solomon, 2001)?

Perhaps your intended audience is classroom teachers or university students who are daily users of the Internet or another known group of computer users. Even better, you may be administering your instrument to a captive audience in a computer lab. If so, access may be a moot point. If not, take the time to know your audience, their level of access, and their comfort level with the technology you intend to use.

Access is *the* central issue in choice of survey mode. If all members of your population or sample do not have equal access to the technology or lack the skills or confidence to respond electronically, coverage error becomes a major concern (Howes & Mailloux, 2001; Solomon, 2001). Coverage error results when some members of the population have zero chance of being included, in this case, our noncomputer users (Dillman, 2007). Internet access is not yet universal, and disparities based on socioeconomic status continue to be a reality (Howes & Mailloux, 2001).

One way to address limited or uneven access is to use a *mixed-mode approach.* For example, one might send online questionnaires for teachers and mail surveys for parents, thus reducing the risk of coverage error. Another option is to offer a choice to respondents: Approach them on the Web and by mail, and offer a choice of response mode—via a Web link or mail. Given a choice of mode, some studies suggest that mail is preferred, and other evidence suggests the reverse (Schonlau et al., 2002). Greenlaw (2006) conducted a study comparing response rates among a group of known Web users of nearly 4,000, divided into three groups: Web based only, mixed mode with respondents having the choice of mode in responding, and mail only. The mixed-mode approach resulted in an improved response rate of 8% over the Web-based-only sample. Responses among the mail-only sample trailed. Similar results using a mixed mode were cited by Schonlau et al. (2002).

In terms of making a decision, it remains the researcher's task to know the audience and select a mode, or modes, that will permit equal access and elicit the greatest return.

Time and Cost

Two frequently touted advantages to Web-based questionnaires are the savings in time and in money (e.g., Deutskens, de Jong, de Ruyter, & Wetzels, 2006; Greenlaw, 2006; Gunn 2002; Solomon, 2001). For the novice researcher, graduate student, or local educator with limited staff and budget, cost is a major consideration. Printing, labeling, stuffing envelopes, and mailing are costly in time and money, as is manual data entry. The prospect of immediate returns and online data is enticing. And what could be more cost-effective or faster than using e-mail for reminders? If cost savings is a primary motivation in considering Internet data collection and access is not an issue, we advise that you consider potential hidden costs: Will you need technical assistance in the design and launching of your survey? Costs of online providers vary according to a number of variables—the more you pay the greater the assistance. Cost can also differ based on the complexity of your design and the automated features you include (Schonlau et al., 2002).

Data Compilation and Analysis

Not only is manual data entry time-consuming and costly, there is also the risk of error. That risk is virtually eliminated when respondents answer on line. Web-based technology also provides for the automatic downloading of the data directly into your data analysis program or spreadsheet. Furthermore, responses completed online are available for immediate and continuous review. This access allows the researcher to assess and monitor the rate of return in "real time." Data downloaded directly into a spread sheet can be "sliced and diced" on a continuous basis, although we remind compulsive researchers that until the final questionnaire has been completed, there are no findings!

The immediacy of return has another potential advantage, as an incentive to respond. Providing respondent access to the summative results "when you complete the survey" may pique the curiosity of some respondents, causing them to complete a survey they might otherwise ignore.

APPLYING DESIGN GUIDELINES TO WEB-BASED QUESTIONNAIRES

Design elements that improve response rates are the same for online surveys as for mail-in versions: an attractive overall design, an interesting first question, a questionnaire that appears short and easy to fill out, an estimate of the length of time required (Best & Krueger, 2004; Dillman, 2000; Solomon, 2001). Transferring these elements with the purpose of online data collection is less than straightforward. For technophiles who are familiar with HTML (hypertext markup language) Code, the prospect of designing online is doubtless irresistible.

For the writers of this book, and perhaps for most of our readers, however, the challenge was different: Proficient though we are with word processing programs, transferring a previously designed survey, the one in Resource A, to the Web via a paid-for subscription with an Internet-based provider was tedious: Limited cutting and pasting, limited choices for placement and scales, and the reduced visual view as we proceeded required patience. On the other hand, the result was not unsatisfactory, and with just a few HTML code rules under our belt (e.g., how to bold and underline), we built a degree of confidence. In the meantime, the following warrant consideration as you contemplate Web design and distribution. Note: Using a professional survey design subscription service and taking advantage of any technical assistance offered may significantly reduce or eliminate many of the risks cited here.

1. Web-based surveys that look attractive on the screen may not be attractive or inviting when printed, particularly if printed in black and white. And they definitely will take more pages. Our two-page Microsoft Word "Modeling the Process" survey became twice that length when we printed the Web-based version. Solution: If you choose a mixed-mode approach, prepare two surveys, one for a mail response and one for a Web response.

2. Screen design requires different consideration than does page design. In effect, every time the respondent "scrolls" down the screen, the page changes. While directions for a single printed page need appear only once, directions for electronic surveys may have to be repeated so that respondents aren't required to "scroll" up. To resolve this problem, we found it necessary to repeat the descriptors for the scale responses for each question.

3. Graphics slow down access (Best & Krueger, 2004; Thomas, 2004). Once more, just because you "can do" does not mean you should.

4. Different Web browsers may alter the appearance of a page. In other words, what your respondents see may not be what you thought that you had sent. The simpler the better (e.g., Gunn, 2002; Schonlau et al., 2002).

5. Directions for successful navigation are essential; frustrated respondents may just give up (Dillman, 2007).

6. Testing your survey on a variety of platforms is highly recommended (e.g., Schonlau et al., 2002).

For specific and detailed descriptions and explanations of e-mail and Web-based design, we direct you to more comprehensive sources, many of which appear on the reference page of this book. One such source is Dillman (2007) who discusses the relative advantages and disadvantages of employing the diverse options in Web designs. We appreciated the list of 13 recommendations for Web-based designs listed in Schonlau et al. (2002)

Skip Patterns

Skip patterns are a sequence of questions that apply differently depending on a respondent's answer to a given question. Here, Web-based design is advantageous.

Suppose you have constructed a different set of questions for parents of primary-grade children and parents of upper-grade children. A paper-and-pencil direction may read, "If you answered 'yes' skip to Item 21, skip Items 22-27 and go to Item 28." Using Web-based design features, the respondent is not even aware that he or she has just "skipped" X number of questions because of a specific answer (Dillman, 2000, 2007; Schonlau et al., 2002; Thomas, 2004).

MODELING THE PROCESS

In our scenario regarding principals' leadership skills, an important demographic variable was secondary versus elementary teacher responses. Using a "skip pattern" we could have directed respondents to 'skip' to a particular question based on how they identified themselves on that variable. For example, "[If you marked A for secondary, skip to question #20. . . ']." In a paper and pencil mode, that takes extra space, giving the questionnaire an appearance of increased length, and respondents don't always "skip" as directed. In electronic surveying, the skip is transparent. The response to the question, "Click on secondary of you teach in Grades 7–12 or click on elementary if you teach in Grades K–6" automatically transfers the teacher to the appropriate new page. The "skip" is seamless.

Though the capacities of the many available Web-based providers vary, as do the costs, there is generally a menu of already-designed question formats and answer patterns: multiple choice, ranking, rating scales, open-ended. And the answer displays can vary: horizontal, vertical, open-ended. Don't be too quick to settle on one or another; try them out and conduct a pilot. Whatever options you incorporate, always be aware of potential limitations resulting from additional cost (yours) or options that tax the capacity of respondents' computers (Schonlau et al., 2002).

CAVEATS AND CAUTIONS

Piloting Your Online Questionnaire

We have previously stressed the importance of piloting or testing your questionnaire with an appropriate audience. The pilot should be in the same mode or modes as you intend to employ for your "real" audience. Launching your online survey takes just one click of your mouse. And once launched, there is no retrieval, although some editing may be possible (and here we speak from painful experience). Taking the time to try it out is well worth it. It may save you more than one sleepless night as you picture your less-than-perfect product moving through cyberspace.

Distribution and Marketing

Prenotification and reminders for online questionnaires can be done via e-mail, mail, or telephone, depending on the access information you have for your respondents. Personalization makes a difference. Generally, e-mail accompanied by a formal letter of introduction suffices for prenotification, but a follow-up in a different mode may improve response rate (Dillman, 2007).

Length of an online document is difficult to judge. As Greenlaw (personal communication, March 2, 2007) observes, "I can't hold the pages in my hand." He suggests providing "indicators of progress" along the way as do others (Dillman, 2007). Findings of a 2000 meta-analysis of 19 Web-based surveys (MacElroy, 2000, cited in Best & Krueger, 2004) support the 10-minute standard. Surveys of 15 to 20 minutes had a "drop rate" (i.e., failure to complete) of 24% to 35% compared with 9% for those surveys requiring only 10 minutes to complete.

Providing preincentives in an online mode presents some challenges, although Best and Krueger (2004) identify several options, including offering cash equivalent incentives or gift certificates or the enrollment of participants in a lottery. Evidence that these incentives actually result in improved responses is minimal (Best & Krueger, 2004; Thomas, 2004). An advantage of online surveys is "real-time" access to results. As observed earlier, providing access to those who complete the survey is a potential incentive in itself. Let them know in advance that when they complete the survey, they will be able to view the results. You may choose to restrict that access with a password.

E-mail

One way to personalize your delivery is to send the survey via e-mail; this approach could increase the response rate. If respondents are not concerned with remaining anonymous, this is certainly an option. Obviously, questionnaires returned via e-mail reveal the sender and provide a written record, which also allows you to follow up individually with those who do not respond. For some school surveys with a known population or sample, this is a credible option.

In most instances, however, we suggest using a URL link, available through online providers.

FINAL THOUGHTS

"To Web or Not to Web" summarized major considerations regarding online surveying: access, cost and efficiency, marketing, and design. We also added some additional "caveats and considerations" as final thoughts. The primary issue and the question that trumps all others is access. Until access to computers and the Internet, and the skills to use both, are universal, access will be the primary limitation in using the Web to gather information. As educational researchers, however, you may have instances when access is not an issue, and the potential of using the Web for efficient gathering and communication of information is not only a viable choice but a preferred choice.

Remember, Web-based technology does not negate the recommendation, throughout this book, to "go slow to go fast." Technology will speed the delivery, return, and analysis of results, but the real work comes prior to launching your questionnaire and is outlined in Stages 1 through 9 in this book.

Since You Asked . . .

Because this handbook is for those who do not work with questionnaires as part of their ongoing professional experience, we have purposely kept the content short and to the point. We have tried to be sequential, emphasizing a step-by-step process.

When preparing this second edition, we realized that things are not the same as they were when the book was first published a decade ago. The climate is different. Technology "begs" to be used. But still, one of our operative words is *simplicity*.

The remainder of this section presents a series of questions, often asked by those involved in a questionnaire activity. Those questions are included here.

How does preparation of an interview form differ from preparation of a questionnaire?

The stages are the same. The advantages and disadvantages of interviews, whether face-to-face or by telephone, are well documented. Interviews allow for in-depth inquiry, resulting in a richness of information not characteristic of questionnaires. However, interviews are time-consuming, and data analysis is difficult because of the wide variety of responses.

With questionnaires, data can be collected from a broader base of respondents, but the information is more shallow. Questionnaires collect less information from more people. With interviews, you typically obtain more information from fewer people. The reason for your study, the Stage 1 guiding questions, and the clarifications done at Stage 2 assist with selecting the best method. For interviews, the three following "rules of thumb" are a good guide for the instrument development process:

1. Ease the data analysis process by formatting the interview instrument in a user-friendly arrangement (see Figure 13.1 on page 73).

2. Data analysis will be more credible if interviews with all respondents are conducted in the same way (i.e., the same wording of initial questions, the same sequence, and the same types of probing questions). Write the interview instrument accordingly.

3. In most interviews, the most valuable information obtained is not the response to the first question but replies to the probing questions after the initial response is given. Therefore, plan to include appropriate follow-up questions in the format of the interview instrument.

We develop the interview form (formally called an "interview schedule") by following these three guiding rules. The interview questions are written in sets, each set focusing on a particular issue. The first question in each set is typically a question that can be answered yes or no.

For example, rather than first asking, "How do you determine what staff development is provided to teachers in your school?" We may ask, "Does your school have a process for determining what staff development is offered to teachers in the school?" This allows for a specific probe—one if the answer is yes and another if the answer is no. We also format the interview instrument to allow for extensive probing. See Figure 13.1, Partial Sample Interview Format With Probing Questions (insufficient response space is allowed in the example shown, but it illustrates the basic structure).

Note that with this format, summarizing the data becomes simplified because you can first quantify the yes/no responses, then cluster similar responses quickly because of their positioning or placement on the interview form.

What is the difference between ranking and rating?

Ranking occurs when you ask respondents to place a set of items in some order, such as order of importance, order of priority, most to least, best to worst, or some such designation. On your questionnaire, the directions for ranking must be very clear.

Say, for example, you have seven areas for possible staff development, and you ask for a *rank* of preference for each of the seven. Write the directions this way:

Below is a list of seven possible topics for staff development at Smith School. Place a 1 beside the item to which you would give top priority. Put a 2 beside the topic that you would give second priority. Continue with a 3, 4, 5, 6, and 7, with 7 for the topic to which you would give least priority.

Not this way:

Below is a list of seven possible topics for staff development at Smith School. Place a 1 beside the item to which you would give top priority. Put a 2 beside the topic that you would give second priority, and so on.

With the last set of directions, many respondents will give 1 or 2 to all seven items; others will give one 1 and one 2 and leave the others blank. When this variety of responses occurs in large numbers, the item is rendered useless.

In the same staff development example, *ratings* are given when respondents use the same scale to address every one of the seven topics. Assume for a moment that

Set 1: 1. Does your school have a process for determining the staff development to be offered to teachers within the school?

If yes
Would you describe the process for me?

If no
Do you have staff development for teachers in your school?

_____

_____

_____

_____

_____

_____

If yes

If no

Do you know how the content was determined? *Go to Set 3*

If yes

If no

How was it done?

Go to Set 2

_____

_____

_____

Do you know if this is the way it is usually done?

If yes

If no

It sounds like this would be your process (recap answer). Do you agree?

Can you describe any other ways that content has been determined?

_____

_____

_____

If yes   If no

Go to Question 2

◄———————   ———————►

2. Has the process for determining the content of staff development been satisfactory?

If yes

If no

Go to Set 2

What do you believe the problem has been?

_____

_____

_____

What recommendations would you make for determining the content of staff development here at school?

Go to Set 2

Set 2:   Have you been satisfied with the staff development program here at school?

If yes

If no

Figure 13.1   Partial Sample Interview Format With Probing Questions

the choices for staff development are, "high priority," "moderate priority," and "low priority." Each one of the seven items would be given one of these three ratings.

The directions may say something like this:

Below is a list of seven possible topics for staff development at Smith School. For each item, indicate whether you believe that item should be given high priority, moderate priority or low priority.

Does coding the questionnaires violate the promise of anonymity or confidentiality?

Remember, there is a difference between guaranteeing anonymity and guaranteeing confidentiality. "Anonymity" means that the respondents cannot be identified by anyone. "Confidentiality," however, promises that nothing a respondent says will be connected to that person. You cannot guarantee anonymity with a coded form. However, if in the introductory letter or in some other place "the small number in the bottom right of the form" is explained, this is acceptable practice. We never code a form without explaining it to potential respondents. Coding in secret is less than ethical research practice.

When is a sample a biased sample? And what's the big deal about random samples?

When surveying, the researcher inquires from an entire population or from a sample of the population. If the sample is representative of the population, it is said to be unbiased. If, however, the sample is not representative, it is a biased sample. If an individual reports information from a biased sample and passes it off as indicative of the population, a grave mistake can be made, especially if decisions will be based on these results. In addition, it is simply unethical to knowingly pass off findings from a known biased sample as true.

Assume for a moment that a school district is considering changing school boundaries. A large group gathers in a school auditorium for a meeting. Attendees complete a questionnaire regarding this issue, and school personnel report to the local newspaper that parents' feelings are such-and-such based upon the results of a survey. What are the chances that the feelings of this group of parents are representative of the feelings of all parents? We undoubtedly have a biased sample: Because not all parents were in attendance, not all parents had an opportunity to respond.

However, if a random sample of parents is selected from among the whole population of parents, and their opinions are surveyed, an unbiased sample results, and (assuming all else was properly done) inferences to the whole population can be made.

If a school surveys those parents who attend open house in the spring and then reports the results as representing parents' attitudes toward that school, let's hope the results are not used for anything important!

If a sample is selected randomly, all members of the population having an equal chance of being selected, *and* the sample is large enough (see next question), then the sample is considered to be representative of the population and is therefore unbiased by definition. When this is the case, results from the sample can be said to be very close to what they would be if the entire population had been queried. Random selection is not a guarantee of population representation, but it is our best chance as researchers.

NOTE: Randomness assumes access. Unless your population is limited to known computer users, randomness is not possible using Web-based surveys alone (Gunn, 2002). Coverage error intervenes. See the section titled "Access" in Chapter 12 (p. 64), "To Web or Not To Web."

> *How large should a sample be, and,*
> *if I mail the surveys, how many must*
> *I get back to be relatively confident of my results?*

There is no direct answer to the sample size question. Sampling is very complex. Otherwise, how could slightly more than 1,000 individuals nationwide accurately predict the outcome of a presidential election within a few percentage points? Suffice it to say that the goal of sampling is to obtain a fair representation of the population. The larger the (random) sample, the more representative it is of the population. Data collected from a sample are not as representative as data collected from the population. Our resource for answering the sample size question is an easily understood article by Daniel Wunsch, published in the *Business Education Forum* in February 1986. He identifies population sizes from 100 to infinity and, depending on how confident you want to be about the representativeness of the sample, states how large the sample should be. Some examples from Wunsch's article are shown in Table 13.1.

Notice the dramatic change in the ratio of the sample size to the population size as the population increases. With a population of 200, responses from two-thirds of the total are necessary if you want the sample to reflect the population within 5%. When the population hits 3,000, the sample size drops to about 11%. Notice the

Table 13.1 Sample Sizes

Population Size	Sample Size (to be confident the data will reflect the population within 5%)	Sample Size (to be confident the data will reflect the population with 10%)
200	132	65
400	196	78
800	260	86
2,000	323	92
3,000	341	94
Infinity	384	96

SOURCE: Wunsch, D. (1986, February). Survey research: Determining sample size and representative responses. *Business Education Forum*, pp. 31–33.

small difference between the sample size with a population of 3,000 and one infinitely large. This difference is only 43.

But watch out! These sample sizes assume a 100% response rate. When your response rate is less than 100%, and it undoubtedly will be with a mailed questionnaire, your sample will always be biased to some unknown degree. The question remains: How many must I get back in order to assume a fair representation of the initial group to whom the questionnaires were sent?

We wish we could offer a number or a percentage as a standard for response rate, but we cannot. Neither does the current research literature offer a clear standard. Researchers understand that larger response percentages reduce the degree of sampling error, hence the attention paid in this book to design elements and other strategies to increase response rate. As a rule of thumb, we are impressed by a response rate of two-thirds or more. If you get less, you might ask, "What evidence do I have that my responses are representative of my population?" Even a relatively low rate (35% to 50%) may be representative if you are able to show that the demographic variables in the returns and those of the population are similar. In a survey of high school English teachers that coauthor Keni Cox conducted some years ago with a stratified sample of approximately 1,100, the response rate was only 45%. On the other hand, the returns replicated the stratification exactly in terms of the most significant demographic variables, hence improving the odds of intended representation.

NOTE: School level surveys with populations as small as 50, or even fewer, are a different matter. Less than 80% would make us nervous.

How do I communicate effectively with the person doing my computer work and keep control of my project?

This brief section is only for those for whom computer work is done by one unfamiliar with the project. That person created the questionnaire data. Primarily its intent is to keep you on the straight and narrow relative to getting from the computer what you need (and avoiding, at least for the moment, getting a bunch of stuff you don't need)

When working with "data people," be sure to . . .

1. Give them your set of guiding questions.

2. Identify which parts of the questionnaire belong to which guiding question.

When the printout is available, sit down and go over every aspect of it with the person who handled the data. Take copious notes and write all over the printout, identifying and labeling those aspects that are important to your guiding questions.

Many individuals, especially those who have a significant statistical background, produce more than is asked for ("I thought this might really reveal something," they will tell you). Although this can be very helpful, be sure to carry out your own plan before wandering into some else's plan. At the same time, do not discount their effort to assist. More often than not, the ideas of one who is knowledgeable will really enhance the quality of your work.

*Are there any special points that are important to know
when sending questionnaires to parents of school children?*

When you ask parents to complete a questionnaire, follow these three rules:

1. Never use anything remotely close to educational jargon in your items. Keep the response formats simple, and keep the form within a 5- to 8-minute time limit to complete.

2. Never refer to "your child" on the questionnaire. Parents may have more than one child in the school or district, and to ask for information concerning "your child" can be confusing for them. We typically ask a parent to answer for the child who has had the most recent birthday (and give a reason for this strange request in the directions). This unusual approach is a form of randomization that we're comfortable with. Never allow parents to choose which child they will respond for. At least never do this in your directions. The respondents will do as they please anyway, but try to guide them so as to produce as random a selection as possible.

3. Establish a strong follow-up plan for nonrespondents. With parents, it often becomes a matter of conjecture as to whether we are hearing from "those who are favorable toward us" or from "those who have an axe to grind." We are uncomfortable with "accepting what we get" when surveying parents—especially when the results will be used as a resource for planning and decision making. Remember, the likelihood of obtaining a fair representation of parents is better when you randomly select 100 and get 85 of those 100 questionnaires back than when you send to all 700 and only get 200 of those returned.

You may believe it is necessary to offer all parents an opportunity to respond ("Why did so and so get a questionnaire, and I didn't?"). This may be an especially strong consideration if opinions regarding a sensitive issue are being elicited. In that case, send to all, but mark the randomly selected sample, and follow up with that group, keeping them separate from the entire set of respondents.

*Are there any special points that are important to
know when sending questionnaires to teaching staffs?*

Of course, when an inquiry is set in motion, it is important to know about any unique situations that could affect the way a particular group answers. This is especially important when considering teacher groups because of the significance of their educational role. Since data from questionnaires report on a situation at one point in time, external incidents can seriously affect responses. For example, when a teachers' union is at an impasse during negotiations, inquiring about attitudes toward the workplace would be foolish. Although external incidents cannot be controlled, it behooves a researcher to plan the data collection process carefully with a view toward minimizing any such influences.

Also, especially when asking teachers about things they would like to see happen in the future, be prepared to respond to their suggestions in some manner. Do not make requests on the questionnaire for information that you are not willing to consider. Questionnaires do not make decisions for you, but neither should anyone be asked questions that will be treated as moot.

*When using scalar responses, how many points
or choices should be offered on the scales?*

While acknowledging that more choices increase reliability (Nunnally, 1978), we are comfortable with a 4-point scale, plus a neutral option, placed at the end. We recommend an even number to discourage a "middle-ground" response—for example, 4 not 5, 6 not 7.

*How do I find a good Web-based
software program/provider?*

Do an online search. Our last Google for "online surveys" resulted in more than two dozen "opportunities" to try it out. And that is what you want to do . . . try them out and compare features, including support and cost. Your local university may have a recommendation. Also, some providers offer an educator discount. Ours does!

CONCLUSION

It seems that almost daily someone reminds us that we are living in the Information Age. For many that statement translates to "doing more, faster," not doing things more easily or doing things better. But we do have a continual need for useful information. Obtaining and using valid information has become a responsibility we all need to assume, not just the "privileged" researcher or the obsessed graduate student.

Obtaining good information and using it effectively is the only way we will continue to improve education. Becoming "data-driven organizations" can be viewed as just another passing thing of the day or as a vital ingredient for improving our profession. Choosing the former is short-sighted. Choosing the latter is commendable but, unfortunately, is only half a choice. The other half is not only emphasizing the use of data but learning how to do it well. Using good data inappropriately or using poor data at all will often lead to more trouble than no use.

Educators in the decision-making process must be skilled in obtaining good information, and questionnaires are one of the data-gathering devices that make this a doable task. Hearing from a lot of people about a lot of things is good practice, not only educationally but politically as well. It is therefore not surprising that use of the questionnaire to gather data is popular.

Unfortunately, many questionnaires (perhaps the last one you tried to complete) are so poorly constructed that the collected data are meaningless and subsequent use of the polluted results becomes an irresponsible act, giving new meaning to the old cliché "garbage in, garbage out."

This book was written in an attempt to help solve this dilemma. Because we want good information—but we don't have an abundance of time in which to collect it—we need a quick but credible process for carrying out the data-collection task. Thus, the nine recommended stages are designed to maximize the accuracy of results with a minimal expenditure of energy.

Your Opinion, Please! is among the few books in print in which there are almost as many pages of examples and resources as there are of text. This is purposeful: One of the most effective (and among our favorite) teaching and learning strategies is modeling. We have tried to provide readers with as many examples and choices as possible.

We hope our suggestions help.

Resource A

Evaluating the Questionnaire

A Self-Assessment

S tages 1 through 7 led you through the steps of questionnaire construction. This three-page checklist is intended for the developer to self-assess the quality of the instrument before formal validation occurs. Much time and energy can be saved if used before proceeding to Stage 8, instrument validation. Poorly written items, omissions, and superfluous content can be discovered in time to adjust with little effort.

Each questionnaire is unique, so some of the listings below may not apply to a particular project. Although most of the items will be relevant to all questionnaires, the researcher must identify which are relevant on a case-by-case basis.

1. General

_____ Is the form pleasant to look at?

_____ Is spacing appropriate?

_____ Are like items grouped together?

_____ Are scales or choice alternatives reprinted on carry-over pages or repeated often enough to be visible at every scroll of the screen?

_____ Is the questionnaire appropriately titled?

_____ Will the form take 10 minutes or less to complete?

_____ Is the use of font sizes, underlining, bold print, and the like done well?

_____ Is the first question engaging, answerable by all, and simple?

2. Questionnaire Content

_____ Is the questionnaire based on the guiding questions?

_____ Have "fuzzy" terms in the questions been clarified/operationalized?

_____ Was an alignment check done?

_____ Have unnecessary items been eliminated?

3. Introduction

_____ Is the questionnaire introduced well, either by a separate letter or as part of the questionnaire itself?

_____ If you were to read the introduction, would you want to complete the questionnaire?

_____ Does the introduction address . . .
__ The purpose of the form?
__ The importance of completing the form?
__ How long it will take to complete the questionnaire?
__ Confidentiality?
__ What will be done with the results?

4. Directions

_____ Are the directions simply written?

_____ Is there a different set of directions for each format change?

_____ Have significant points been emphasized (but not overemphasized)?

_____ Do respondents know what to do with a completed questionnaire?

5. Quality of Items

The 12 criteria down the left side are the screens to determine the quality of each item. Identify the questionnaire items across the top and place a check mark in each box where the questionnaire item meets the criterion.

	Item Number														
Criterion[a]	1	2	3	4	5	6	7	8	9	10	11	12	13	14	15
1. Simple construction and word order															
2. Common, well-defined terminology; **no jargon**															
3. Asks only what respondent knows															
4. Respondents not led; no "hard" or "soft" terminology															
5. No compound questions															
6. Sensitive questions carefully worded; self-indictment avoided															
7. Negative responses can be interpreted															
Scalar Response Items															
8. Scale descriptors fit item (especially important)															
9. Equal intervals between choices, semantically and spatially															
10. "Undecided" response kept off the scale															
11. No absolutes (e.g., use of the words, *all* or *never*)															
12. No double qualifiers (use of qualifiers in both the item and the response)															

a. See Stage 3 for clarification of criteria.

Resource B

Sample Introductions

Following are sample questionnaire introductions that have been used by various school districts. The following examples, although not models, give ideas for addressing those involved in educational issues.

TO PARENTS: EXAMPLE 1

Our Board of Education is studying the success to date of the XYZ Reading Improvement Program being conducted in 13 school districts geographically close to ours. The program is operating in the school that your child in Grade 4 attends. Many parents know about this program, but others have not yet found out about it. No matter how much you know about the program, you are encouraged to answer the questions presented on the following two pages. Parents' feelings about school programs are important considerations in making program decisions.

The selection of parents to receive this form was random. Thank you for your cooperation and interest in the educational programs in our school.

TO PARENTS: EXAMPLE 2

It is very important that parents have a chance to tell how they feel about what is being taught to their children. When parents' feelings are known, it will help our schools make plans to provide the best possible education.

Below are some questions to help us get needed information concerning the middle school that your child (or children) attends. Please answer exactly the way you feel. You are not asked to put your name on this paper or on the return envelope that is enclosed. Your answers will be grouped with those of other parents to give a general picture of how parents feel.

Thank you for taking your time to give the needed information and for helping to improve your neighborhood school.

TO TEACHERS

For those needy students enrolled in our special reading program, you are a very important person. These children have had a history of reading difficulty, and through your efforts, and the efforts of others, something is being done. A commitment has been made, and it needs to be followed through in the best way possible.

Because of your involvement, your feelings about various aspects of the special reading program and your suggestions for improvement provide important information. Program strengths and problems that you have encountered need to be documented. In this way, plans for the future of the program can be made.

The purpose of this activity is to get your input regarding these issues. It is estimated to take about 10 minutes to complete this form.

Your anonymity, of course, is absolutely guaranteed. Your cooperation is greatly appreciated in this activity. Results of this inquiry will be sent to you when they become available.

TO PRINCIPALS: EXAMPLE 1

The Classroom Management Through Information project is being used by five of our schools in an effort to improve the overall reading program. Because of the instructional leadership that building principals provide, their perceptions are very important to future decisions regarding the project.

Please take a few minutes to respond to the statements and questions on this form. The information obtained from this instrument will be helpful to the project staff and to the administrative staffs in each of the schools. Complete anonymity of response is guaranteed. You will receive a report of findings when the data are analyzed and a report has been written. Thank you for your help.

TO PRINCIPALS: EXAMPLE 2

We believe that more children can be directly affected with a major emphasis on staff development than in many other ways. The XYZ Reading Improvement Program, focusing on staff development, is one of the strategies our district is using to improve the overall reading program.

What you have to say concerning the impact that the XYZ program has had on you in your daily efforts is very important information. You are familiar with the present strengths and weaknesses, can assess its potential, and no doubt, have suggestions for its improvement.

The accompanying form is provided for this purpose. The few minutes you take to contribute your input is important to our school district, to you, and ultimately, to your staff and students.

Complete anonymity of response is guaranteed. When the results are known, you will be among the first to receive feedback. Your cooperation is greatly appreciated.

Resource C

Sample Directions and Formats

The following samples show different types and styles of directions and formats that have been used in questionnaires for various school districts. These samples, along with those in the prototype questionnaire, give you a wide variety from which to choose for your own use.

The reasons to consider varying your formats are twofold: First, with creative formats you may be able to obtain more information in less space and with less effort on the part of the respondent. For example, getting three or four pieces of information from one line of questionnaire text can be quite advantageous. Second, because questionnaires are so common, a unique format may encourage potential respondents to cooperate. If your questionnaire can look a bit different from the rest, you perhaps stand a better chance of having it returned. You are encouraged to be creative in your efforts, but *never sacrifice clarity and simplicity*.

The examples that follow show a variety of ways to elicit responses. Saving space without sacrificing the amount of data collected or ease of response is the main focus of the examples. *The intent of this section is to demonstrate format, not content.*

Bear in mind that *there are pluses and minuses for each kind of format*. Note the following:

- Space savers may be accompanied by increased complexity of format. It is always dangerous to sacrifice simplicity.

- Space savers may limit the variability of response. Example 1 collects four pieces of information per item (that is good!) but at the same time limits each response to one of three alternatives. (This is potentially a problem if a full range of response is important, as it usually is in a research project.)

- Unique formats can appear very busy, without enough white space. This crowding may communicate complexity to the respondent, even though the response pattern is actually simple.

- Unique formats may be accompanied by unnecessarily complex directions. Be especially careful when writing directions for unfamiliar formats.

EXAMPLE 1

Directions: Below are listed the units of the staff development program for the XYZ Reading Improvement Program. For each of these units you are asked four questions:

1. Regardless of how well it was presented, *how important do you think the content of the unit is* with regard to improving the teaching of reading in the classroom?

2. *How effective was the session* for that training unit?

3. *How useful has each of the training units been for you* as a resource teacher?

4. *What need do you have* for additional inservice in each area?

Be sure to make four marks for each unit, one for importance, one for inservice effectiveness, one for usability, and one for future inservice need.

1. Self-Assessment: A Tool for Changing Behavior

Importance			Effectiveness of Inservice			How Useful for You			Future Inservice Needed	
Very	Somewhat	Not Too	Very	Somewhat	Not Too	Very	Somewhat	Not Too	Yes	No

2. Interpretation of Test Data

Importance			Effectiveness of Inservice			How Useful for You			Future Inservice Needed	
Very	Somewhat	Not Too	Very	Somewhat	Not Too	Very	Somewhat	Not Too	Yes	No

3. Grouping for Instruction

Importance			Effectiveness of Inservice			How Useful for You			Future Inservice Needed	
Very	Somewhat	Not Too	Very	Somewhat	Not Too	Very	Somewhat	Not Too	Yes	No

EXAMPLE 2

Eight activities to assist low-income families are listed below. Please place one check for each activity to indicate whether you (1) have been directly involved, (2) are only familiar with the activity, or (3) have little or no knowledge of the activity.

Involved	Familiar	Know Little	
_____	_____	_____	Activity 1: Cluster closed-circuit television (CCCTV)
_____	_____	_____	Activity 2: Computer-assisted instruction (CAI)
_____	_____	_____	Activity 3: Mobile instructional laboratories
_____	_____	_____	Activity 4: Outdoor education and camping
_____	_____	_____	Activity 5: Horizons Ahead
_____	_____	_____	Activity 6: Field experiences
_____	_____	_____	Activity 7: Health services
_____	_____	_____	Activity 8: School-community identification

EXAMPLE 3

Directions: Considering the manner in which the Read to Learn program has functioned this year, indicate the degree to which the program has afforded you the opportunity for the following:

	Great Opportunity	Somewhat	Little or No Opportunity
1. To develop a formal diagnosis of each student's needs			
2. To prescribe instruction for each student			
3. To collaborate with other classroom teachers			
4. To use classroom techniques designed to improve students' self-concepts			
5. To receive administrative support for the program			
6. To receive inservice training necessary for successful program operation			
7. To use those instructional materials accompanying the *Read to Learn* program			

EXAMPLE 4

Below are listed some statements, each of which may or may not describe the Read to Learn program. Read each statement and, according to the following choices, indicate your opinions about the Reading to Learn program by circling the appropriate response.

1 = A very descriptive statement

2 = A somewhat descriptive statement

3 = Not a descriptive statement

nc = Not certain

Circle your choice

1	2	3	nc	1. Children are generally interested in this program.
1	2	3	nc	2. Materials are appropriate for the level of instruction.
1	2	3	nc	3. There is too much teacher preparation.
1	2	3	nc	4. The program is too expensive.
1	2	3	nc	5. Children are capable of learning with this system.
1	2	3	nc	6. The program makes it difficult to stay organized
1	2	3	nc	7. Extensive inservice training of teacher is necessary.
1	2	3	nc	8. Parents seem supportive of the program.
1	2	3	nc	9. The program is worthy of continued support.
1	2	3	nc	10. The program blends well with the regular reading program.

EXAMPLE 5

Directions: You will be provided with the objectives of this professional development session. For each objective, consider (a) how well you understood the content and (b) how valuable you think the information will be for practical classroom use. Then use a scale of 4 (positive) to 1 (negative) to indicate your answer for each of the objectives. Place an x in the spaces that best indicate your opinion. Make certain there are two marks for each objective, one for understanding and one for practical value.

	A				B			
	Degree of Understanding				*Degree of Practical Value in the Classroom*			
	Very Well ⟵⟶ *Not Well*				*Very Valuable* ⟵⟶ *Not Valuable*			
Objectives	*4*	*3*	*2*	*1*	*4*	*3*	*2*	*1*
1								
2								
3								
4								
5								

EXAMPLE 6

Below are listed four major objectives of the XYZ reading program. Considering your experience with the program this year, indicate the extent to which you think each objective has been met. For each objective, place a check in the column that best expresses your feeling.

Objective Attainment

Objectives	*Met very well*	*Generally well met*	*Not met too well*	*Not met at all*
1. To stimulate an interest in reading that will motivate teachers to set new levels of expectation and will motivate pupils to try hard to reach these levels				
2. To extend teachers' understanding of the essential elements of a good program of developmental reading				
3. To reinforce, review, or introduce specific techniques for motivating students to read.				
4. To involve parents and community in volunteer activities, informational meetings, and other supportive efforts contributing to the total program thrust				

EXAMPLE 7

Part 1: Information about the new reading program

Directions for Teachers: Read each question below and put a check (✓) in the space under the answer you choose. Sometimes it is difficult to select an answer. If this should happen, choose the one that expresses how you feel *most of the time*.

The scale represents varying intensities of feelings. The endpoints are more intense feelings, whereas those nearer the center are less so.

1. In general, are you pleased with the reading program?

YES!	Yes	yes	no	No	NO!

2. Do you believe the reading program, as currently designed, is meeting the needs of the limited-English students?

YES!	Yes	yes	no	No	NO!

EXAMPLE 8

Suppose that you had a chance to select strategies to *help improve the reading program in our school district.* Several may be considered. How seriously would you consider those listed below? Place a check in the box that is closest to the way you feel for each of the three strategies.

	I would give serious consideration	I would give some consideration	I would give little or no consideration
1. More instructional materials to increase the variety of literature with which students work			
2. Training of teachers to help them improve their teaching of reading			
3. Additional help in the classroom to allow for more individual attention to students			

If you were to pick ONLY ONE, which would it be? (circle your choice)

1   2   3

EXAMPLE 9

Below are listed six elements of the XYZ Reading Improvement Program. You may know about some elements and not others. For *each element* answer two questions by making two marks.

    A. How much knowledge do you have of each of the six XYZ elements?

    B. How satisfied are you with each of the six elements listed?

Do not check the second set if you do not know about the specific part.

XYZ Elements	*A. How much knowledge do you have of this part?*			*B. If you have at least some knowledge, how satisfied are you with the part?*			
	Quite a bit	*Some*	*Little or none*	*Very satisfied*	*Satisfied to a degree*	*Not satisfied*	*Not certain*
1. The XYZ student outcomes							
2. XYZ materials available to help teachers with reading instruction							
3. The XYZ benchmark assessments							
4. The XYZ inservice program							
5. The role of the XYZ reading resource teacher							
6. XYZ reading materials used in the classroom							

EXAMPLE 10

Directions: Below is a list of questions dealing with issues that are important to the operation of our school. Read each question and decide how you generally feel about the item. *Be sure to give your overall impression rather than allowing one or two isolated incidents (good or bad) to affect how you answer the question.*

Each question has four choices. Check the box that comes closest to your feelings. Make your choices from among the following alternatives:

"Definitely yes"

"Generally yes"

"Generally no"

"Definitely no"

	Definitely yes	Generally yes	Generally no	Definitely no
1. Do you believe you have opportunities to obtain additional skills you may feel you want or need?				
2. Do you believe your assigned work responsibilities are fair and reasonable?				
3. Do you believe you have opportunities to express any concerns you have?				
4. Do you believe you get recognition for your performance and accomplishments?				

EXAMPLE 11

Directions: Below is a list of questions for which your answers are important to the operation of our school. Read each question and decide how you generally feel. Be sure to give your overall impression rather than allowing one or two isolated incidents (good or bad) to affect how you answer the question.

A scale from 6 = *Definitely Yes!* to 1 = *Definitely No!* is shown below. Place the number that comes closest to your answer in the blank.

Definitely		*Marginal*			*Definitely*
Yes!		*Yes*	*No*		*No!*
6	5	4	3	2	1

Rating

_____ 1. Do you believe you have adequate opportunities to obtain additional skills you may feel you want or need?

_____ 2. Do you believe your assigned work responsibilities are reasonable?

_____ 3. Do you believe you have adequate opportunities to express any concerns you have on the job?

_____ 4. Do you believe you get adequate recognition for your performance and accomplishments?

Resource D

Critiquing a Questionnaire

Finding Flaws

This resource contains a questionnaire and our critique. The original instrument has some incredibly obnoxious errors as well as some that are more subtle and difficult to detect. The critique contains our assessment—we did not try to be all-inclusive. Careful readers of this book may well find additional items to criticize; don't be misled into thinking that ours is the final word. Your own critiques of the forms, we are sure, will be equally valid. It would be a good idea to reproduce Resource A, The Evaluation Checklist, to assist you.

FINDING FLAWS

Scenario: *The following questionnaire is intended for use in XYZ School. Parents' overall attitudes are being assessed. The data collected will serve as the baseline for future planning.*

PARENT QUESTIONAIRE

Introduction: School XYZ is conducting a parent survey. It is important that you answer the following questions. A high response rate is necessary if we are to know how parents feel.

Part 1

Directions: A scale divided into five parts is shown below. Each part represents a degree of parent perception about different parts of the school program. For each statement, mark the column that comes closest to representing your feelings.

	Definitely yes	*I think so*	*Not sure*	*I don't think so*	*Definitely no*
1. I am pleased with my child's progress in school.					
2. Discipline should be more strict than it is now.					
3. I favor the open classroom concept.					
4. Teachers in School XYZ seem extremely interested in the students.					
5. There is need for more instructional materials in the school.					
6. I feel the school should stress fair play and good sportsmanship.					
7. People of the community are tiring of the traditional practices of the district.					
8. My children seem to enjoy school.					
9. Teachers should concentrate on teaching and not spend time taking role, collecting lunch money, and being on duty.					

10. Communication from school to home needs tremendous improvement.					
11. It is important to teach attitudes and values at school.					

12. Do you think parents should improve the   Yes_____
quality of the children's education by volunteering   No_____
to work in the classroom?

Part 2

Rank the following needs in the order of importance that you feel they should be addressed.

Rank   *Need*

1. There is a need to improve the school library.   ____

2. There is a need to offer after school aesthetic   ____
   experiences to students.

3. There is a need to build an obstacle course for   ____
   use in physical education.

4. There is a need to create a teacher's resource center where   ____
   they can obtain extra instructional materials for classroom use.

5. There is a need to obtain materials to implement the career   ____
   education program.

Part 3

Briefly state how well you feel that School XYZ is doing toward providing a quality educational program.

CRITIQUE OF THE QUESTIONNAIRE

How many of the following problems did you identify?

- The term *questionnaire* in the title is misspelled and should not have been used in the first place. Poor title.

- Poor introduction. There is nothing here to encourage participation.

- Part 1: Directions are not good. The word *perception* may not be appropriate for a parent questionnaire and is incorrectly applied. How about *attitude* instead?

- Part 1: The 5-point scale does not contain equal intervals. There is too much semantic space between *Definitely* and *I think. I think* really means not sure.

- Item 1: Which child? In what academic area? This leaves the respondent saying "It depends on whether . . ."

- Item 2: Unclear! Discipline where and for whom? At home? At school? In general?

- Item 3: Too much leeway for interpreting the open classroom concept. "Open classroom concept" is educational jargon.

- Item 4: There is a double qualifier: *extremely* in the question, *definitely* in the response.

- Item 5: Respondents are asked a question in an area for which they cannot be expected to have knowledge.

- Item 6: This is a leading question and will yield little information. How can anyone possibly be against *fair play and good sportsmanship?*

- Item 7: *Traditional* is a hard word. The item leads the respondent.

- Item 8: Confusing and too general—maybe some do and some do not.

- Item 9: The question is leading the respondent. It implies a disproportionate amount of time is already being spent; *roll* is misspelled.

- Part 1: The scale is not repeated on the new page.

- Item 10: There is a double qualifier: *tremendous* in the question, *definitely* in the response.

- Item 11: Compound question: attitudes and values are two different things; values are a very sensitive issue and to present the item in this context can be explosive. Careful!

- There is an unnecessary format change between Items 11 and 12, poor spacing and a leading question (how can anybody be against anything that improves the quality of children's education?). It also assumes that parent volunteers will provide the improvement.

- Part 2: *Ranking* needs to be explained. The heading words, *Rank* and *Need,* are reversed. Generally, these are not things to which parents should be asked to respond. They imply solutions to problems rather than getting at the problems themselves. Items 4 and 5 are not parent oriented. Words such as *aesthetic* are not appropriate. The word *teacher's* in Item 4 should be *teachers'*.

- Part 3: Poor choice of format. It will be very difficult to summarize and analyze the data.

- There is no indication that Part 3 is the end of the questionnaire; there are no directions on what to do when completed.

Resource E

Modeling the Product

Stages 1 Through 7

This resource shows the progression of the first seven stages of the questionnaire development process for two different scenarios.

SCENARIO 1

As a result of state funding, regional training centers for school leaders have been established, and the director is conducting a needs assessment to determine the most desirable structure and content for the centers. A questionnaire will be sent to individuals in local school districts who would be potential participants or who would advise others within their respective districts to participate.

Stage 1: Establish the Guiding Questions

1. How do current school leaders feel about the need for professional development and what is their interest level in becoming involved, personally or as an organization?

2. How would school leaders structure such a professional development program?

3. What is the attitude of current school leaders toward professional development sessions that they have attended in the past?

4. What are potential topics for coverage?

5. Are there differences of opinions among individuals according to selected demographic categories?

Stage 2: Operationalize the Guiding Questions

Question 1: This question is straightforward; there appears no need for clarification.
Question 2: The word *structure* needs to be operationalized. In this case, *structure* shall relate to

(a) Grouping of participants, (b) scheduling of activities, and (c) possible work between sessions

Question 3: The phrase *attitude of current school leaders* shall deal with (a) practicality, (b) opportunity to reinforce the learnings, (c) interest, (d) coverage of content, and (e) quality of the sessions.

Question 4: Topics for which selections/ratings will be made are (a) program accountability, (b) curriculum, (c) instructional strategies, (d) administrative policies and practices, (e) school climate, (f) leading school reform, (g) supervision and evaluation of teachers, (h) maintaining a safe school environment, and (i) working with special interest groups.

Question 5: The term *selected demographic categories* shall include (a) district size; (b) level of school—that is, elementary, junior high, or senior high; (c) job category; and (d) years of experience in job category.

Stage 3: Write Items and Format Responses

Stage 4: Design the Questionnaire

Stage 5: Write Directions

Stage 6: Categorize Respondents

The questionnaire presented on the following pages represents an initial effort at design. Stages 3, 4, 5, and 6 created only a draft, because the alignment check (Stage 7), which will recommend revisions, has not yet been done.

PROFESSIONAL DEVELOPMENT FOR TODAY'S EDUCATIONAL LEADERS: WHAT ARE YOUR THOUGHTS AND IDEAS?

As you are aware, recent funding has become available to establish training centers statewide in which educational leaders can participate. If this opportunity is to be fully realized, the organization and operation of the centers must fit the interests, needs, and schedules of those participating.

This inquiry allows you the opportunity for input on a variety of issues regarding the centers. Please respond with your candid opinions. If you were "leader for a day," how would you structure the centers?

With this activity, you are helping establish the plan that will determine how the centers will operate.

Part 1 Directions: Below is a set of statements *relating to professional development for today's school leaders.* Indicate your degree of agreement with each statement by circling your category of response. Use the following marking scheme:

> SA = Strongly agree
> A = Agree
> D = Disagree
> SD = Strongly disagree
> NC = Not certain

1. A professional development program specifically geared to today's educational leaders is necessary.　　SA　A　D　SD　NC

2. If it fits your particular needs, you personally would become involved in such a program.　　SA　A　D　SD　NC

3. If it were designed well, you would support your district's involvement.　　SA　A　D　SD　NC

4. Some form of follow-up between sessions is necessary to assist in putting professional development content into practice.　　SA　A　D　SD　NC

5. Small collegial groups that meet between sessions are a good way to interact and assist each other in putting content into practice.　　SA　A　D　SD　NC

6. Assignments (reasonable in length) between sessions should be an element of the professional development program.　　SA　A　D　SD　NC

7. It is better to concentrate on a few conceptual areas in a year rather than addressing several important areas but limiting the coverage.　　SA　A　D　SD　NC

Part 2 Directions: Below are listed various kinds of groupings for training. Rank each grouping pattern based on your preferences. Give a rank of 1 to the one you most prefer, a rank of 2 to the next preferred, and so on to 4 for the least preferred. *If you would not choose to participate in professional development activities because of any specific grouping, write VETO in the blank.*

Rank

_____ A group of individuals within the same organization (school or district) with no others in attendance

_____ A group of individuals with similar jobs (principals, lead teachers, assistant principals, district office staff, etc.) with no others in attendance

_____ A group of individuals with need for a specific kind of skill development (e.g., communication, school reform, curriculum, accountability, etc.)

_____ A completely heterogeneous (mixed) group of individuals

Part 3 Directions: How do you feel about certain training strategies for skill development, especially in light of your daily work load? Your response options are the following:

Fine	*OK but have reservations*	*No*

Please put a check mark in the column that best fits your feelings.

	Fine	OK, but have reservations	No
1. Planning your *personal* professional development program with input and assistance from your supervisor			
2. Reading assignments (of reasonable length) between sessions			
3. Writing assignments (of reasonable length) between sessions			
4. Assigned follow-up activities in which you apply a specific competency to current job situations			
5. Having trainers, other participants or other peer coaches provide on-site individual assistance			
6. Contracting with the training center to do certain things during the year (similar to student classroom contracts)			

Part 4 Directions: Below are listed the proposed topics for coverage in the first round of the professional development program. These topics would be covered in a 2-year period. For each of the areas answer two questions:

1. How important is the topic to today's educational leaders?

2. As you observe educators today, *generally, what is their current knowledge/skill level?*

Circle the number that comes closest to your opinion. Consider each item independently of the others, and *try not to give the same rating too many times*, especially in the importance column.

1 = Extremely important
2 = Moderately important
3 = Not too important

1 = High skill level
2 = Moderate skill level
3 = Skill level definitely needs improvement

1	2	3	1. Understanding and promoting program accountability in the organization	1	2	3
1	2	3	2. Facilitating curriculum development	1	2	3
1	2	3	3. Promoting a variety of instructional strategies	1	2	3
1	2	3	4. Understanding administrative policies and practices	1	2	3
1	2	3	5. Creating a positive school climate	1	2	3
1	2	3	6. Leading school reform	1	2	3
1	2	3	7. Supervising and evaluating teachers; working with the less than satisfactory employees	1	2	3
1	2	3	8. Maintaining a safe school environment	1	2	3
1	2	3	9. Managing change in education	1	2	3
1	2	3	10. Working successfully with parents and the community	1	2	3

Part 5 Directions: Please check the items that describe your situation. This information will be used only to describe the responding group and to compare group responses.

Your work site	*Your job category*	*Years of experience in your job category*
___ High school	___ Principal	___ 1–3
___ Junior high/middle	___ Assistant principal	___ 4–7
___ Elementary	___ Director/coordinator	___ 8–15
___ District office	___ Assistant superintendent	___ 16 or more
	___ Superintendent	

Part 6 Directions (optional): If you have additional comments or suggestions regarding the regional training centers, briefly state them on the back of this page.

> Thanks for your time. Mail the completed form
> in the enclosed stamped, self-addressed envelope.

Stage 7: Conducting the Alignment Check

Initially, Stage 1 and Stage 2 questions and clarifications directed the Stage 3 development process. Stage 7 cross-references the guiding questions and the questionnaire items to determine if all bases are covered, as well as whether any items on the proposed questionnaire are unnecessary because they do not address any of the guiding questions. The alignment check for Scenario1 is shown below. The guiding questions are subdivided and the operationalized definitions from Stage 2 are shown down the left side. THE ITEMS SHOWN IN **BOLD** IDENTIFY EITHER OMISSIONS IN THE QUESTIONNAIRE OR QUESTIONNAIRE ITEMS THAT ARE NOT NECESSARY BASED ON THE GUIDING QUESTIONS AND THE OPERATIONALIZED DEFINITIONS.

Questionnaire Items

Guiding Questions Plus Operational Items	Part 1	Part 2	Part 3	Part 4	Part 5		
	1 2 3 4 5 6 **7**		**1** 2 3 4 5 **6**	1 2 3 4 5 6 7 8 **9 10**	Work Site	Job Cat.	Years Exp.
1. How do leaders feel?	x x x						
2. How to structure?							
Grouping participants		x					
Scheduling activities							
Work between sessions	x x x		x x x x				
3. **Attitude toward past activities?**							
Practicality							
Reinforce learning							
Interest							
Content coverage							
Quality of sessions							
4. Topics for coverage?							
Accountability				x			
Curriculum				x			
Instructional strategies				x			
Policies/practices				x			
School climate				x			
Leading reform				x			
Supervision/evaluation of teachers				x			
Safe environment				x			
Working with special interest groups							
5. Demographic categories?							
District size							
Level of school					x		
Job category						x	
Yrs. experience							x

The initial alignment check showed that Guiding Questions 1 and 2 were being covered, Guiding Question 3 was missing from the questionnaire altogether, Guiding Question 4 was being covered (except for working with special interest groups), and three of the four demographic categories were addressed. District size was not asked.

Also, some items on the questionnaire were not included in the guiding questions and therefore may be considered unnecessary. These include Part 1, Item 7; Part 3, Items 1 and 6; Part 4, Items 9 and 10. You can determine this by moving directly down from the numbered questionnaire item on the chart. There are no x's in the column for these items. Also, the right-hand column calling for assessment of skill level in Part 4 is not needed. Nothing in the guiding questions asks for this.

The questionnaire developer has some decisions to make at this point. If the questionnaire is to be mailed, it is already long enough. In fact, it may be too long. To add items relating to Guiding Question 3, without eliminating something else, would be a bad decision. If this situation were "for real," consider eliminating Guiding Question 3 altogether. It seems the least important of the five, and besides, it may be something we can easily find the answer to another way. Adding district size to the demographic section, however, would not be a problem.

Finally, because concern about the length of the form is an issue, we would propose that it be shortened, especially if a high rate of return is needed. Establish priorities on what information is essential, reduce the guiding questions or simplify the Stage 2 process, and get the questionnaire into a two- to three-page document. For example, Part 1 could be cut to the first three items; Part 2 could stay, and Part 3 could be eliminated because it is more specific and the intent of this inquiry is to determine the overall attitudes of potential participants. Part 4 is important, but skip Items 9 and 10 and the measurement for skill level on the right side, and make it one-dimensional. Part 5 must stay.

A section like Part 6 (already noted as optional) is typically included and need not align itself with any particular question.

We acknowledge that there is not a reader under the sun who, when reaching this point of the book, would actually spend time to meticulously attend to the above issues as part of their learning. The reason it was included was to give a gestalt to the process and to make the actual alignment activity meaningful. While this step of questionnaire development may appear cumbersome and therefore—given the workload of the developer—not necessary, we implore you not to skip it. As has been stated, if you make errors in development (which we all do) and distribute the questionnaire, the errors cannot be corrected. This is the step to find those errors.

SCENARIO 2

School District XYZ, as part of its overall accountability plan, needs input from recent high school graduates regarding their after-the-fact perceptions of the high school experience. During the previous year's graduation activities, students completed a postcard indicating their willingness to participate and an address label containing the "probable address" to which a brief questionnaire could be sent.

Stage 1: Establish the Guiding Questions

1. What were the graduates' feelings about the overall quality of their school?

2. What were their feelings about how well the school did in preparing them for the future, whatever those plans might be?

3. What were their feelings about the staff at the school?

4. Were there differences of opinions based on gender? Course of study in high school? High school attended? Current activity?

5. What did the students like best and least about the school?

Stage 2: Operationalize the Guiding Questions

Question 1: This will be a holistic assessment in which "the eye of the beholder" is the focus. Thus, no clarification will be made.

Question 2: "Feelings about preparation" will focus on (1) what they are doing presently and (2) a career.

Question 3: "The staff" will be (a) teachers, (b) counselors, and (c) administrators. "Feelings" will be translated into (a) support and (b) expectations.

Question 4: "Course of study" will be (a) college or (b) other than college; "current activity" will be (a) full-time job, (b) trade or vocational school, (c) community college, (d) 4-year college, (e) military, or (f) other.

Question 5: This will be open-ended, student choice.

Stage 3: Write Items and Format Responses
Stage 4: Design the Questionnaire
Stage 5: Write Directions
Stage 6: Categorize Respondents

The questionnaire that follows is an initial design effort. It will need to be revised after the alignment check (Stage 7) has been completed.

LOOKING BACK TO MY HIGH SCHOOL YEARS (HOW DO I FEEL ABOUT MY HIGH SCHOOL, NOW THAT I'VE GRADUATED?)

To the Graduates from _____ High School:

It has been almost a year since your graduation from _____ High School in the XYZ School District. We at the school hope your lives have been successful since you left us. In order for us to continuously improve our programs for students, we would like to hear from you. How do you feel about _____ high school a year later? Did you enjoy the experience? Did we prepare you for what you are currently doing? We really want to hear.

You indicated on a postcard at the end of last year that you would be willing to give us your input. This very brief form will tell us how you feel, what strengths you observed, and what you would suggest to correct some of our shortcomings.

Your responses will be anonymous. We *will not know* who completed the forms. Thank you for helping in this important activity. Results of this inquiry will be available on www.XYZDistrict.com, hopefully by June 1.

Thank you for your time.

_____, Principal

Section A: If you were to give your high school an overall grade, what grade would you give? **Circle the grade** you would give your school.

A   B   C   D   F

Section B: Below are listed several things that **contribute to or detract from** the quality of one's high school experience. These would be the things that perhaps caused you to give the grade that you did. As you look back on your experience, indicate whether you believe each of the items was a PLUS for you or a MINUS. A **PLUS** is a strength and a **MINUS** is a weakness. Check the column on the right that best describes your feelings.

In most cases, your responses would be "some plus . . . some minus." Answer the way that you generally feel. Do not allow a few specific instances to affect your overall rating.

	Definite PLUS	Somewhat a PLUS	Neither a PLUS nor a MINUS	Somewhat a MINUS	Definite MINUS
1. Appropriate, challenging courses					
2. Teachers expecting me to achieve					
3. Preparation for what I am currently doing					
4. Fairness of grading					
5. Knowing what career I wanted					
6. Support from teachers					
7. Adults who would listen to me					
8. Learning to be personally responsible and self-disciplined					
9. Friendly, supportive students					
10. Course offerings that I wanted					
11. The way the school dealt with drug and alcohol problems					
12. Extracurricular activities					

Section C: Complete the following three sentences. *PLEASE DO NOT USE PEOPLE'S NAMES.*

1. The thing I liked BEST about the school was _____
   _____

2. The thing I liked LEAST about the school was _____
   _____

3. If I could change one thing about the school, it would be _____
   _____

Section D: Please complete each of the following items. The items are included to assist in more accurately reviewing the information.

1. Your gender: _____ Male

   _____ Female

2. What was your basic course   _____ Preparing for college
   of study in high school?   _____ Preparing for other than college

3. How have you spent most of your time after graduation?

_____ Working

_____ Trade or vocational school

_____ Community college

_____ Four-year college

_____ Military

_____ Other (specify)_____

> Thank you very much for your time. Place the
> completed form in the attached self-addressed,
> stamped envelope and mail.

Stage 7: Conduct the Alignment Check

Considering each of the guiding questions:

1. *What were the graduates' feelings about the overall quality of the school?*
   This is directly addressed in Section A, with specifics being addressed in Section B.

2. *What were their feelings about how well the school did in preparing them for the future, whatever those plans might be?* (Operationalized to include "the present" and "career.")
   This is addressed in Section B, Items 3, 5, 8 and peripherally in Item 10.

3. *What were their feelings about the staff at the school?* (Operationalized to include teachers, counselors, and administrators; feelings to include support and expectations.)
   This is addressed in Section B, Items 2, 4, and 6 for teachers, and Item 7 for all adults. ***Administrators and counselors are not addressed***. Is this important? If not, skip it, because we do not want more than one sheet, both sides, and would not like the format in Section B to run over to the back side.

4. *Were their differences of opinions based on gender? Course of study in high school? School attended? Current activity?*
   The ability to answer this question is covered in Section D plus the customized letter in the introduction that identifies the school.

5. *What did the students like best and least about the school?*
   Section C addresses this.
   Section B, Items 9, 11, and 12 do not directly address the five guiding questions, although they are interesting and could relate to the overall quality issues.

References

Best, S. J., & Krueger, B. S. (2004). *Internet data collection.* Thousand Oaks, CA: SAGE.

Deutskens, E., de Jong, A., de Ruyter, K., & Wetzels, M. (2006). Comparing the generalizability of online and mail surveys in cross-national service quality research. *Marketing Letters, 17*(2), 119–136. Retrieved January 5, 2007, from www.springerlink.com/content/5537111073w15756/fulltext.pdf

Dillman, D. A. (2000). *Mail and Internet surveys: The tailored design method* (2nd ed.). New York: John Wiley.

Dillman, D. A. (2007). *Mail and Internet surveys: The tailored design method* (2nd ed., update). New Jersey: John Wiley.

Greenlaw, C. (2006, November). *A comparison of Web-based and paper-based survey methods: Testing assumptions of survey mode and response cost.* Paper presented at the annual meeting of the California Educational Research Association, Monterey.

Gunn, H. (2002, December). Web-based surveys: Changing the survey process. *First Monday, 7*(12). Retrieved March 28, 2007, from www.firstmonday.org/issues/issue7_12/gunn

Hager, M. A., Wilson, S., Pollak, T. H., & Rooney, P. (2003, June). Response rates for mail surveys of nonprofit organizations: A review and empirical test [Abstract]. *Nonprofit and Voluntary Sector Quarterly, 32*(2), 252. Retrieved January 3, 2007, from http://nvs.sagepub.com/cgi/content/abstract/32/2/252

Howes, C. M., & Mailloux, M. R. (2001). Comparing two survey research approaches: E-mail and Web-based technology versus traditional mail. *Journal of Marketing for Higher Education, 11*(4), 51–66.

Huang, J. Y., Hubbard, S. M., & Mulveny, K. P. (2003, February). Obtaining valid response rates: Considerations beyond the tailored design method. *Evaluation and Program Planning 26,* 91–97. Retrieved January 3, 2007, from www.sciencedirect.com.libproxy.fullerton.edu/science?_ob+ArticleURL&_udi=B6V

Nunnally, J. C. (1978). *Psychometric theory* (2nd ed.). New York: McGraw-Hill

Schonlau, M., Fricker, R. D., Jr., & Elliott, M. N. (2002). *Conducting research surveys via e-mail and the Web.* Santa Monica, CA: RAND.

Solomon, D. J. (2001). Conducting web-based surveys. *Practical Assessment, Research, & Evaluation, 7*(19). Retrieved January 3, 2007 from http://pareonline.net/getvn.asp?v=7&n=19

Strike, K. A., Anderson, M., Curren, R., van Geel, T., Pritchard, I., & Robertson, E. (2002). *The ethical standards of the American Educational Research Association.* Washington, DC: AERA.

Thomas, S. J. (2004). *Using Web and paper questionnaires for data-based decision making.* Thousand Oaks, CA: Corwin Press.

Wunsch, D. (1986, February). Survey research: Determining sample size and representative responses. *Business Education Forum,* pp. 31–33.

Index